GIVE ME A "J"!

It's All about Jesus

ARTHUR BLESSITT

LEGACY
PUBLISHERS INTERNATIONAL

Give Me a "J"!
It's All about Jesus

ISBN 1-880809-49-4

Copyright © 2006 by Legacy Publishers International
Legacy Publishers International
1301 South Clinton Street
Denver, CO 80247
www.legacypublishersinternational.com

Prepared in association with Edit Resource (www.editresource.com)

Front Cover and Back Cover photos by Dave Talbot
Talbot Photography - Denver, CO - (303) 777-1926

2 3 4 5 6 7 8 9 10 11 / 09 08 07

I dedicate this book to my adorable and wonderful wife, Denise Irja Blessitt. She has traveled the world with me in more than 250 countries as we shared Jesus together on every continent. She is a godly woman whose heart overflows with the love of Jesus. This love is evident as she shares Jesus with others, and it makes her the most effective witness I've ever met.

CONTENTS

PREFACE

"Give me a 'J'!"

"J!"

"Give me an 'E'!"

"E!"

"Give me an 'S'!"

"S!"

"Give me a 'U'!"

"U!"

"Give me another 'S'!"

"S!"

"What's that spell?"

"*Jesus!*"

One thing I'm known for is leading the Jesus cheer. It not only gets a crowd excited, but it also gets us focused on what's most important: Jesus.

Give Me a "J"! is a book about how to share Jesus with the people we meet every day. Its central point is very simple: in sharing with others for their salvation, all we really need to do is tell them about Jesus. There's no evangelistic process to memorize, no need to be an expert in theology, no pressure of any kind. This is something every single follower of Jesus can do—and can love doing.

I am filled with excitement in presenting this book to you, because I know firsthand the thrill of seeing people born into the kingdom of God. Welcome to the privilege of doing something you can be sure is the will of God— helping people come to know Jesus as their Savior!

~

This is something every single follower of Jesus can do—and can love doing.

~

Living on a farm in the American South, I received Jesus as my Savior at the age of seven. The very next day, I began sharing about what had happened to me and how my friends could know Jesus. In the years since, this lifestyle of being a witness of Jesus has taken me around the world.

For a number of years, I was known as the "minister of Sunset Strip," leading a Jesus coffeehouse in West Hollywood, California. I spoke on stage at nightclubs and rock festivals in the late 1960s and early 1970s. I was part of the Jesus movement that swept the United States and the world. During that time, I learned to communicate the message of Jesus in areas where people had rejected church.

After being called by Jesus to carry a twelve-foot cross on foot across America, I learned to speak person to person with critics, doubters, and the eager. Then Jesus called me to carry the cross in every nation on earth. I have since carried the cross on foot in 305 nations, island groups, and territories. By the grace of God, I have walked more than thirty-seven thousand miles—listed in the Guinness World Records as the world's longest walk.

In this journey with the cross, I have spoken about Jesus with people in every nation, and He has led me to share Him in ways that touch the heart. With an approach of love and kindness, and using terms that do not provoke anger but rather arouse interest, I have shared with people of every religion and have led many to know Jesus as Savior and Lord.

My life of sharing Jesus includes being the guest speaker at Harrods, the world's most famous store in London, England, where I spoke every hour for an entire day. In addition, I spoke to the staff at the Bank of England, to detectives at Scotland Yard, and at private receptions with royalty. I have spoken to prayer groups in the U.S. Senate and House and also at the Pentagon. I have spoken to tens of thousands in the Rose Bowl, the Orange Bowl, JFK Stadium, Wembley Arena, Trafalgar Square, and Hyde Park.

From Westminster Chapel in London to the Crystal Cathedral in California, I have seen the world open up to the message of Jesus. From meeting with Yasser Arafat in war-torn Beirut to Prime Minister Begin's house in

Israel to the presidential palace in Egypt, the cross and I have been welcome. From the roadsides of India, with tens of thousands lining the highways to welcome the cross, to the jungles of the Amazon, I have seen the hunger of the world for the glorious news of Jesus Christ.

There's nothing special about me. In many ways, I'm no different from the boy who grew up amid the cotton fields. It's the message about Jesus that's so powerful, that gets so much attention, and that changes lives forever.

Certainly I realize that God may not call you to share about Him as widely in the world as I have. But I know that in your daily course of life you come up against many who need to know Jesus. Your family, your friends, and others in your community can come to know Jesus as Savior and Lord as you simply tell them the truth about Jesus.

Follower of Jesus, be released by the Holy Spirit and start today to lift up Jesus in word and deed in every way possible that honors Him. He once said, "The harvest truly is plentiful, but the laborers are few. Therefore pray the Lord of the harvest to send out laborers into His harvest" (Matthew 9:37-38). And that is my prayer for this book—that it will empower laborers to go into a world ripe for harvest.

Glory! I can see a flood of people coming to know Jesus, and even now I can hear heaven rejoicing.

Give me a "J"!

PART 1

IT'S ALL ABOUT JESUS

1

SHARING JESUS IN THE TWENTY-FIRST CENTURY

We do not preach ourselves, but Christ Jesus the Lord.

—2 Corinthians 4:5

My walk around the world started with a walk across America, beginning on Christmas Day of 1969. I was living in Hollywood, California at the time, and God called me to take the wooden cross off the wall of our His Place building, where it had been hanging and where I had been preaching, and carry it to Washington, D.C., by way of New York. The walk itself was glorious. And then, after carrying the cross across America in 1970, the next year I felt led to return to New York and lead a mighty outreach in Times Square.

But what happened? At first I stood there in Times Square preaching as loudly and as forcefully as I could, while thousands of people walked by, but nearly everyone ignored me. The thoughts running through their minds seemed to be, *Oh, another street preacher yelling at me. I've heard it all before.* And they would hurry on.

I knew something was wrong. Here were people who needed Christ, but plainly I was not communicating with them in an effective way. So one evening I said to the ten people who were with me, "Let's just sit down right here and pray." So we sat down under a little tree, joined hands, and started to pray out loud.

~

Here were people who needed Christ, but plainly I was not communicating with them in an effective way.

~

And guess what happened next? Although my eyes were closed for prayer, I thought I could hear a crowd begin to gather around this circle of people who were praying on the ground. I confess that I peeked for a moment, and there were people all around us—hundreds of people! They were trying to see what was happening and overhear what we were praying about.

Finally I ended the prayer and started to share about Jesus. People listened. Then I grew overconfident and stood up and started to preach. What happened next? The crowd left—I had turned back into a street preacher, in their minds. But then I sat back down and started talking to the ten fellow believers, and a crowd gathered again.

So for the next three months, that's what we did. We sat under that little tree in Duffy Square and Times Square and we shared Jesus. We ran a microphone cord in the tree branches so that people in the crowd could hear better what we were saying. But we didn't preach; we simply talked with each other and with the people around us about Jesus. During those three months, many thousands chose to follow Jesus.

I learned a valuable lesson in New York back in 1971: don't preach *at* people; share *with* them. That makes all the difference.

"SHARING WITH"

Sadly, many followers of Jesus still take the "preaching at" approach. They point a finger and say, "You're a sinner. You need to repent or you're going to hell." Usually, all this does is to make the preacher appear self-righteous and cause other people to become defensive. It turns them off from even considering Jesus.

And so I pray that we will put the "preaching at" approach behind us once and for all. I pray that, in the twenty-first century, the followers of Jesus will learn to share Him with others in a comfortable, positive, and effective way. When people see Jesus, the Spirit convicts them and they are drawn into the Kingdom by God's love.

Is this biblical? Oh yes! Jesus Himself sent out His followers two by two into the towns and villages of Israel, instructing them, "Whatever house you enter, first say, 'Peace to this house.' And remain in the same house, eating and drinking such things as they give" (Luke

10:5, 7). That's a beautiful picture of getting up next to unbelievers, spending time with them, and sharing Jesus with them in a nonconfrontational manner.

Were we trying to get people to buy into a religious system, they might become offended. Were we trying to persuade people of the superiority of our moral beliefs, they might become hostile toward us. But what I am talking about in *Give Me a "J"!* is simply talking about Jesus and leaving the other stuff alone.

All around the world, I have found that I can talk to almost anybody about Jesus—His life and teaching and mission in the world. When Jesus is shared with love, with joy, and with excitement, people are open to talking about Him and receiving Him into their hearts. It can happen with you, too.

FEAR NOT

Not long ago, I was speaking with a wealthy woman who lived in Florida. She told me that she was afraid to respond to Jesus' call to share Him because she thought it would mean going to some grimy city street and hanging out with the homeless and other people who were nothing like her.

I told her not to worry. She did not need to share Jesus on urban streets unless she sensed God calling her to that kind of ministry. She could share Jesus with people she met at the country club, at the garden club, and anywhere else her normal round of activities took her. With those people, she could be very effective for Christ.

Like this woman, many people have fears about sharing Jesus. And to these people, I say, relax! Sharing Jesus is merely talking about someone you love—Jesus—with whomever you happen to meet. Our attitude should be that of sharing our best friend with other friends. This is how we normally talk as we share treasured experiences in our lives.

Imagine that you have been on a terrific vacation and afterward you have returned to your job. You would want to tell your coworkers all about your vacation, wouldn't you? Sure! Because you had a great time and want to share that experience with them.

That's what it's like in sharing Jesus. We love the Lord, and so we tell others about Him and invite them to know Him too. That's it.

This approach eliminates many of the worries that people have.

- *You can be yourself.* I have my own style of sharing Jesus that works for me, but you don't need to copy my style or anybody else's. Share in whatever way fits with your personality and preferences. We all have the same goal: to share Jesus effectively so that others will ask Him into their heart. But we don't have to do it in the same way.

- *There's no script to follow.* I know that some evangelists will encourage others to follow a certain pattern every time they present the gospel. That may work well for some people, and certainly when it does, I am glad that it has helped someone to receive new life in Jesus. But my approach is different. There is nothing rote about it. All I do is encourage my fellow believers to share Jesus however seems most appropriate for the person they are with, as they are led by the Spirit. In this way we cover the same fundamentals but we tailor the approach to the individual with whom we are speaking.

• *There's no risk of failure.* In sharing Jesus, all we are doing is issuing invitations to follow Him. The power to change lives doesn't lie with us but with the Holy Spirit. We encourage people to commit their lives to Jesus, but it is never up to us to make that decision for them. So no matter what their response is, we have not failed. The only failure lies in not being faithful to share Jesus in the first place.

Take heart. In the rest of *Give Me a "J"!* you will see how sharing Jesus can be comfortable and relaxed and can fit into your everyday life. We can share Jesus in ways that people understand, using the kind of language that people are speaking, and showing a love that others can feel. Then Jesus will draw them to Himself while we watch and cheer Him on!

AUTHORIZED, COMMISSIONED, EMPOWERED

But maybe you are not convinced yet that you should even be sharing about Jesus. That's for other people, you might think.

The biblical evidence says otherwise. The glorious mission of every follower of Jesus—male or female, young or old—is to share about Him and lead people to believe in Him, repent of their sin, and follow Him. And because we have the scriptural command to share Jesus, we can be sure that God is with us as we speak on His behalf. This, too, casts out fear.

Jesus set the example of what He has asked us to do. Declaring His personal mission statement, Jesus said, "The Son of Man has come to seek and to save that which was lost" (Luke 19:10). In other words, His purpose in coming to the earth was to earn our salvation through His death on the cross and to share with people the message of how that salvation could be applied to them personally through trusting in Him.

~

Jesus set the example of what
He has asked us to do.

~

And Jesus made good on His claim. Luke 8:1 says, "[Jesus] went through every city and village, preaching and bringing the glad tidings of the kingdom of God." He spent most of His time traveling about so that a maximum number of people could meet Him and have an opportunity to follow Him.

Now, here's the next step: Jesus asks us to do what He did. He said to His followers, "As the Father has sent Me, I also send you" (John 20:21). That is, He passes on to us the mission given to Him by the Father to go to people and share with them how to receive the new life He offers. Just like Him, we are to seek and save those who are lost.

The basis of this command to us is Jesus' own authority as the Son of God. "All authority has been given to Me in heaven and on earth," He asserted (Matthew 28:18). Therefore, we have His authorization to share the message of salvation in Jesus. This gives us a boldness in sharing.

Many times, as I carry the cross in countries where public preaching and proselytizing are not allowed, a police officer, soldier, or other official will ask me, "Do you have permission to do this?"

I reply, "Yes."

"From where?"

"At the top."

Frequently, that ends it, as my interrogator assumes that a chief of police or president or someone like that said I could carry the cross in their country. But what I mean is that my authority comes from the *very* top—from Jesus Himself.

And then, in addition to Jesus' authorization, we also have His commission. It is a universal one. "Go therefore and make disciples *of all the nations*" (Matthew 28:19, emphasis added). "Go into all the world and preach the gospel *to every creature*" (Mark 16:15, emphasis added). That doesn't leave out anybody, does it?

We don't just have Jesus' permission to share about Him; we have His commission. We are *commanded* to do so. Now, I realize that only certain people, including myself, have the spiritual gift of evangelism (Ephesians 4:11). But that's not what Jesus was talking about. He wants *all* His followers to be His witnesses on a regular basis. Just as not all believers are pastors but all of us are ministers, so not all of us are evangelists but all of us are witnesses.

Finally, in addition to Jesus' authorization and commission, we also have His empowerment. He promised, "You shall receive power when the Holy Spirit has come upon you; and you shall be witnesses to Me in Jerusalem, and in all Judea and Samaria, and to the end of the earth" (Acts 1:8).

We are not sent out alone to persuade people to follow Jesus by employing our own eloquence and reasoning ability. We're not outwitting anybody. We're not winning debates. No. Jesus said, "Lo, I am with you always, even to the end of the age" (Matthew 28:20), and He *is* with us through the Spirit. He will convict and convert sinners as we share with them the simple message about Him.

Jesus' earliest followers did just as He had told them. "Daily in the temple, and in every house, they did not cease teaching and preaching Jesus as the Christ" (Acts 5:42). And in time their sharing of Jesus went much farther than just their hometown. After a period of intense persecution in Jerusalem, "those who were scattered went everywhere preaching the word" (Acts 8:4).

We go too. We go to those around us—to our family, to our friends, to our business colleagues, to service people and sales clerks, to people we meet on business trips, vacations, and mission journeys. Wherever we go, we tell people about the Jesus we love.

We have been authorized, commissioned, and empowered by Jesus to tell people the good news about salvation. It's a privilege—and it's not hard or intimidating when we look at it simply as sharing Jesus with our friends and acquaintances.

NOT LIFESTYLE ALONE

Now, I know there are many people who say evangelism is about a lifestyle, not about what we say. These folks will claim, "I live it; I don't speak it."

One man had been with the same company for fifteen years, and he had wanted his life to be a witness for Jesus on the job. Finally somebody came up to him at work and said, "There's something special about you, something unusual about you."

This made the man feel really good. He thought, *Fifteen years I've been showing my light and waiting for this. Finally it's here. Somebody has figured out I'm a follower of Jesus.* He said, "What have you noticed about me?"

The other person asked, "Are you a vegetarian?"

By all means, live a life that is consistent with what you profess to believe. And should your lifestyle catch the attention of others and give you an opportunity to share Jesus with them, that's great. But please don't rely upon your lifestyle alone to witness for Jesus; that's not enough.

The apostle Paul, speaking of unbelievers, wondered,

How then shall they call on Him in whom they have not believed? And how shall they believe in Him of whom they have not heard? And how shall they hear without a preacher? And how shall they preach unless they are sent? As it is written: "How beautiful are the feet of those who preach the gospel of peace, Who bring glad tidings of good things!" (Romans 10:14-15)

Somebody's got to speak. Paul was right—assuming we don't speak, how will anybody know who Jesus is and how they can be saved in Him?

As we have seen, Jesus passed His mission on to us. And how did He describe that mission? "The Spirit of the LORD is upon Me," He declared, "Because He has anointed Me to preach the gospel" (Luke 4:18). The Greek word translated "preach" means "to herald forth" or "to proclaim." So you and I are to follow Jesus' example in sharing about Him in words.

A REVOLUTION IN THE MAKING

Sharing Jesus is His idea. It is Jesus who told us to go. It is Jesus who is with us. When we lift up the name of Jesus, it is He who does the drawing of people to Him. It is Jesus who saves and comes into one's life. It is Jesus we will spend eternity with. It's all about Jesus.

Did you know that, since you have Jesus as your Savior, you have already met the sole qualification required for those who will share Him with others?

Did you know that most people with whom you might speak about Jesus would be fascinated to learn about Him?

Did you know that most people have *never* been prayed for personally, and as you offer to pray for them, it can melt their hearts?

Everywhere I have gone, I have found people open to hearing about Jesus. And so, after traveling throughout the entire world, I am optimistic, not pessimistic, about people coming to Jesus. In fact, I am more excited today than I have ever been about sharing Jesus with the people of the world. As Jesus said, the harvest is ripe; the only question is whether enough laborers will head out into the field to reap it (Matthew 9:37-38).

I believe that in our day a revolution is at hand as Jesus followers are released, in the name and power of Jesus, to go everywhere and talk with everybody about Him. It's simple but so important. And oh, the joy that is waiting for us as we take part in God's great work in the world!

There is one thing you can do on earth that you can know will bring rejoicing in heaven, and that is leading someone who is lost to find new life in Jesus. This brings rejoicing and celebration in heaven (Luke 15).

Fear not. Jesus is with you. And the cross has gone before you. I know, because I have carried it into every nation where you might go.

The call is clear. The Spirit is with us. Let's go, go, go!

∽∽∽

QUESTIONS TO CONSIDER

- How has this chapter opened your eyes to misconceptions you may have had about sharing Jesus?

- What is holding you back from sharing Jesus more consistently and more boldly?

- What ideas are already forming in your mind about how you can share Jesus better?

2

PASSION
FROM ABOVE
TO SHARE
JESUS
ON EARTH

*Behold, I say to you, lift up your eyes and
look at the fields, for they are already white
for harvest!*

—John 4:35

efore I started walking around the world with a
cross, I led His Place, a Jesus nightclub coffeehouse on Sunset Strip in Hollywood, California.
One evening, a couple of men got into an argument at
His Place and one of them—a three-hundred-pound fellow named Henry—hit the other man in the face. Hit him
so hard, in fact, that an ambulance had to come and pick
up the injured man.

I went up to Henry, put my arms around him, and
said, "Henry, why did you hit that guy?"

Henry didn't answer. He just acted uncomfortable and glanced around at the others standing nearby.

Thinking some privacy was called for, I said to Henry, "Come in the office."

He stepped into my office. And do you know what happened next? This huge, broad-shouldered, tough guy fell over in my arms, crying. Through his tears he at last answered my question: "He was laughing at my girl-friend, who's in jail."

I learned something that day. However tough or otherwise immune some people might seem on the outside, on the inside they need God's love just as much as anybody else. Henry was a three-hundred-pound baby with a hurting heart. And just like him, many people whom we might write off by saying, "Oh, they won't respond to the message of Jesus," are in fact ready to respond to the Lord if encouraged by us even a little.

We need to look at people, not with a worldly or selfish perspective, but with the eyes of Jesus. We need to speak to the heart of a person and not to his or her appearance.

FROM COMPASSION TO HARVEST

How did Jesus look upon people? With love and compassion for all. The Lord is "not willing that any should perish but that all should come to repentance" (2 Peter 3:9). He wants every lost person to come into the family of God.

Oh, how He yearns for the ones who are wasting their lives apart from His love! Looking over the holy city one day, Jesus said, "O Jerusalem, Jerusalem...how often I wanted to gather your children together, as a hen gathers her chicks under her wings!" (Matthew 23:37). As a shepherd searches for a lost sheep, as a woman searches for a lost coin, and as a father welcomes home a lost son (Luke 15), so Jesus has come "to seek and to save that which was lost" (19:10).

One Gospel passage says this of Jesus: "When He saw the multitudes, He was moved with compassion for them, because they were weary and scattered, like sheep having no shepherd." What did Jesus do next? He turned to His disciples and said, "The harvest truly is plentiful, but the laborers are few. Therefore pray the Lord of the harvest to send out laborers into His harvest" (Matthew 9:36-38).

From compassion to harvest, that is Jesus' pattern, and it should be ours as well. And so, how about us, do we have the same yearning as Jesus has for the lost? Do we look upon the lost with compassion, such that we can't wait to share Jesus with them?

~

From compassion to harvest, that is Jesus' pattern, and it should be ours as well.

~

In my experience, too many believers are not sharing Jesus at all or are sharing far too little. Some of us may just need some encouragement or some teaching about how to share Jesus with others. This book can help with that. But for the most part, it really is a heart problem: we need to be filled with the compassion and love of Jesus so that we love the lost as Jesus does.

I don't know the condition of your heart, and I wouldn't presume to judge you. But I do recommend that you ask God to search your heart and reveal to you what needs to be changed. Then ask Jesus to change you by the power of the Holy Spirit. Jesus will give you the desire to share Him with others.

THE DESIRE TO SHARE JESUS

God gives the desire to share Christ enthusiastically. That desire comes from the heart of God. All we have to do is ask for the desire. The apostle John assured us, "If we ask anything according to His will, He hears us" and answers our prayer (1 John 5:14). The desire to share Jesus with others is unquestionably God's will for us.

Paul told us that "we have the mind of Christ" because the Holy Spirit reveals truth to us (1 Corinthians 2:14-16). The Holy Spirit will also give us the *heart* of Christ—when we ask for it. The heart of Christ is a heart filled with love and compassion for all, including the ones who are stumbling in spiritual darkness apart from the light of Christ.

My daily prayer is this: "Lord, take out of me anything that doesn't look like Jesus. Put in me everything that looks like Jesus." It's all about Jesus and having His heart for the lost.

I continue in prayer, "Lord, purify my heart. Help me feel like You feel. Help me see people the way You see them. Move me in Your likeness." As God fills our hearts with love and compassion for the lost, He will begin moving us into the world to share Jesus with those who need Him.

I like to say that followers of Jesus need to be *insulated* from the world but not *isolated* from it. Certainly we don't want to allow ourselves to get caught up in the sinful things that are going on in the world, but like Jesus dining with tax collectors and sinners, we need to go where unbelievers are. We must be in the world but not of it, wise as serpents and innocent as doves.

What's keeping us from moving among unbelievers to share Jesus? Walls of our own making. Some of these walls are internal ones—keeping us from sharing Jesus with others. Others are external—keeping us from going where certain groups of people are. Let's look first at these external walls.

THE CROSS OVER BERLIN

In the summer of 1981, I was carrying the cross through West Germany. I timed it so that I arrived in West Berlin for a rally called Berlin for Jesus, held at the Olympic stadium. (West Berlin was located within what was then known as communist East Germany.) About fifteen thousand people gathered at the stadium on Saturday, June 6, to worship and listen to a series of speakers, including me, sharing about Jesus.

I spoke for fifteen minutes, and at the end of my message I said, "This stadium was built by Hitler to commemorate the 1936 Olympics. It was built to glorify man. There was a flame lit to commemorate the start of the Olympics. In just a moment I am going to take this cross and carry it across this field, up the steps, and we are going to raise the cross above where the torch burned. I pray that those who hunger and thirst will be filled with the fire of the Holy Spirit."

Everyone on the speakers' platform was stunned, since I had told my plans to none of them. But I didn't let that stop me: I stepped off the stage, took the cross, and started walking across the playing field. By this point, everyone in the stadium was roaring. People were standing, clapping, and praising God. I reached the other side of the stadium and began to climb the steps—up, up, up.

At the top, by prior design, I met my Swiss friend Johannes Czwalina. We helped each other up onto the platform where the torch had been lit for the 1936 Olympic Games. As we lifted the cross, people exploded in praise and tears. The cross was raised high above Berlin. It was one of the most glorious moments I have ever lived.

A REVELATION FROM GOD

As I stood at the highest point of the Berlin stadium with the cross, stretching to the eastward were eight thousand miles of atheistic communism, all the way across Eastern Europe and Russia and China to

Vietnam. I knew I was called by Jesus to go with the cross into those areas.

West Berlin was located in communist East Germany. The highway from West Germany to West Berlin was lined with a fence and security installations. Drivers had to stay on this road and not leave it to go into East Germany.

A few days after the rally, my daughter Gina, who was my driver, was with me when our car broke down just inside the East German border. We had the cross tied on top of the car. I prayed for God to fix the car's problem, but He did not. In vain we tried to repair the car or get it towed into West Germany. Gina and I had to spend the night beside the highway in the camping trailer we towed behind the car.

At midnight, lying on the floor of the trailer, I was still praying. "God, You have me here for a purpose. What is it?"

Then I felt the Lord speak to me. "Arthur, you've been praying about when to carry the cross behind the Iron Curtain. Well, I don't have an Iron Curtain. There are no walls. The walls are in your mind."

God had finally gotten through my hard head. The term "Iron Curtain" is a political term, not a biblical term. In 1946, in a speech in Missouri, Winston Churchill said, "An iron curtain has descended across the Continent." And so preachers began to preach, and teachers began to teach, that we should go into all the world except the communist world, because it was now impossible to share Jesus there. The wall of communism and the "Iron Curtain" had closed these nations. Like others, I had believed this, even after twelve years of carrying the cross around the world.

I said, "Lord, *walls* and *Iron Curtains* are terms that are gone from my vocabulary, except to use when I'm preaching or when I write about them." And I have gone on to carry the cross in every communist nation as well as every other nation on this earth. Glory! Jesus did it!

WALLS IN OUR MINDS

The iron curtain is in our minds. It is an iron curtain of disbelief and imagined impossibilities. We merely *think* that certain places and certain people are off-limits for sharing Jesus.

Communism has collapsed in most of the world, but now we have militant Islam. And so we talk about the "10/40 window" and we hear people say, "You can go anywhere and preach, but you can't go to Muslim countries." Do you understand what we're doing? We're building walls that keep people from hearing the gospel.

People have often asked me something like this: "Arthur, when you went to Libya, did you feel the demonic power in that country, with Muammar Gaddafi running it?"

I say, "No. Everywhere I go I feel the glory of God, because He's with me." I feel the Father, Jesus, and the Holy Spirit. As a matter of fact, in Libya, Gaddafi paid for all our expenses and sent an airplane to fly my son and me to see him in the middle of the desert; so much for that country being an off-limits place.

Let me tell you, I have carried the cross and preached in every one of the Middle East nations. In 1998, when Saddam Hussein was still in power, officials of his government invited us into Iraq. Some years earlier, in 1980, I spent the night in Prime Minister Menachem Begin's house in the Sinai and kept my cross in his house overnight when I was carrying it from Jerusalem to Cairo.

~

The walls are all in our minds.

~

The last sovereign nation I carried the cross in was North Korea, the most closed and rigidly atheistic nation on earth. Yet in 1998 I carried the cross there and prayed for the North Korean people. The government gave us our invitation to enter in a red velvet folder.

The walls are all in our minds.

But we don't need to talk about communism or Islam to find our external walls. We put up walls in our own cities, our own neighborhoods, even our own homes. Some people have external walls of racism: they won't witness to people of certain ethnic backgrounds. Some have walls of education: they won't witness to their doctor or anyone else who is better educated than they are. Some have walls of lifestyle: they won't share Jesus with homosexuals or drug addicts or the country club set or whoever it may be. Some people have walls of relationship: they will witness to strangers but won't share Jesus with members of their own family.

In each case, we have drawn circles and said, "We'll go everywhere except *there*." Our excuse might be that the people on the other side of the wall are too hard to reach. Or we might even admit to ourselves that we are just too biased or too scared to go there.

Each of us must ask ourselves, again and again, what external walls we have erected in our minds. And they may not look like an iron curtain at all; they may look more like glass—we may not at first see them or be aware that they exist. But they are there and we need to figure out what they are. Why? Because to the extent that we let the walls remain, we are limited in how we can share Christ.

The Lord may not call us to witness for Him in the Muslim world. But then again, He may. And certainly He may call us to share about Him with people who make us uncomfortable for one reason or another—people who look different from us, who have different values from ours, or who have a different lifestyle from the way we live. Will we dare to say no to Him; after all He has done for us?

The external walls must come down. As we open ourselves up to God and change our way of thinking, we will discover that these walls will come down, just as the "Iron Curtain" evaporated for me as soon as by God's grace I realized that it really didn't exist.

FAILURE AFTER FAILURE

In addition to the external walls we put up, there are internal walls. These are ways we disqualify ourselves from sharing Jesus with others. We may cheer others on as they share Jesus, even pray that God will pour out His Spirit on them, but we do not share ourselves, because we think we have been eliminated from service.

Over the years, I have heard all sorts of reasons given for not sharing Jesus with others. Actually, I think they are more excuses than reasons. The excuse I hear most commonly is *"I've failed."*

More specifically, people will say, "I've been divorced" or "I've had an abortion" or "I used to preach and then backslid." They have drawn a circle around themselves and have disqualified themselves, so that they no longer have a responsibility to God and to others. It's excuse making to keep from doing God's will.

We need to get over our fears. Should someone mention your past, you can just say, "Yes, I've messed up things in my life. But Jesus has changed me. He's at work in me now, and I praise Him. I'm not your Savior, anyway—Jesus is. And He loves you." The point, as always, is to bring the discussion back to Jesus.

~

We need to get over our fears.

~

Now, some may say, "Well, it's not just that I messed up in the past; I've still got a problem." They say, "I still smoke" or "I still drink too much" or "I slept with my boyfriend just last month." And so they eliminate themselves on that basis. What should people caught in a pattern of sin do?

As it turns out, these people have a lot in common with the prophet Isaiah. When this prophet first encountered the holiness of the Lord God, he cried out,

Woe is me, for I am undone!
Because I am a man of unclean lips. (Isaiah 6:5)

He felt unworthy because he knew he was a sinner. But God purified his lips by sending an angel with a hot coal. Then Isaiah heard the Lord say,

Whom shall I send,
And who will go for Us?

And Isaiah responded, "Here am I! Send me" (verse 8).

If you are involved in sin, do like Isaiah. Admit that you are doing wrong and seek God's forgiveness for it— He is eager to give it. And when He does, He will still call you to serve Him. Say yes. It's that simple. Repent, turn from your sinful ways, and go on to serve God.

What we need are saved sinners filled with the power of the Holy Spirit who say, "I'm not proud of my sins. I'm not proud of the failures of my life. But oh, glory to God, I've been washed in the blood of Jesus, and I'm going to the whole world to tell about Him and to live for Him."

God has mercy for and uses sinners. Don't follow up a failure of morality with a failure of obedience.

THE INADEQUACY OF OUR INADEQUACIES

While a sense of personal failure is the most common reason people give for disqualifying themselves from the call to witness, it is not the only one. Let me mention a few of the others, in case you might find your own attitude reflected in any of these internal walls.

- *"I'm too ugly." "I'm too fat." "I'm too old." "I'm the wrong color." "I'm uneducated." "I'm a woman."* This is a sampling of the ways in which some people think their personal appearance or condition eliminates them from helping to lead a person to Jesus.

  Here's the truth: how you look doesn't matter as much as the condition of your heart. A person full of the love of Jesus and with a smile on his or her face and filled with the Holy Spirit is a powerful witness for Jesus. Forget about yourself. Think about Jesus and about His love for the lost. It's all about Jesus; what matters is Him. God made you the way He wants you to look—so forget about it and go and share Jesus with others.

- *"I'm not an extrovert."* Some people evidently think that being more quiet by nature means they are not equipped to share Jesus. But you don't have to be an extrovert to share Jesus.

  Consider this. You are quiet and mild, but as you pass a home, you see smoke and fire coming from it. Suddenly you change. You run to the house screaming to wake up the sleeping people inside. You also call 911. What made you change? The people you can possibly save!

- *"I don't speak well."* Some people lack confidence in their speaking ability. This was one of the excuses Moses used when the Lord called him to service. "O my Lord, I am not eloquent, neither before nor since

You have spoken to Your servant; but I am slow of speech and slow of tongue" (Exodus 4:10). What did the Lord have to say about that?

"Who has made man's mouth?" asked God from the burning bush. "Or who makes the mute, the deaf, the seeing, or the blind? Have not I, the LORD? Now therefore, go, and I will be with your mouth and teach you what you shall say" (verses 11-12).

God is the one who does the converting. It's the power of Jesus, not the words you use in telling about Him, that changes men's and women's souls. Trust God. He will give you words to say that will be effective as He uses them.

Whatever your internal wall might be—a past failure, disappointment in your appearance, a quiet nature, a lack of speaking ability, or anything else—God will use you. In spite of everything you are, He'll say, "I've chosen you. You're Mine. I like you just the way you are. Now let's go."

∽

It's the power of Jesus, not the words you use in telling about Him, that changes men's and women's souls.

∽

The treasure of the good news of Jesus resides in we earthen vessels (2 Corinthians 4:7). When we are weak in our own abilities, then we are strong with God's power (12:10). Our inadequacies are inadequate to disqualify us from witnessing for Christ.

Identify the internal walls that are keeping you from sharing Jesus as you should. You may want to write them down on a piece of paper. (You don't have to show it to anybody.) Then deal with them by putting them under the blood of Jesus and saying, "Lord, cleanse me." Get it clear and start over.

Internal walls, just like external ones, have got to come down in the name and in the power of Jesus. In the freedom of Jesus, you can be an effective witness of Him to others.

TEAR DOWN THIS WALL!

On June 12, 1987, in a speech delivered at Berlin's Brandenburg Gate, President Ronald Reagan famously demanded, "Mr. Gorbachev, tear down this wall!" In November 1989, just two years later, I was in East Germany with my son Joshua when the Berlin Wall actually did come down. I chipped pieces out of it myself. And I know that if that wall between East and West could be torn down, so can be the walls that keep us from sharing Jesus in certain places or with certain people. You can break out and be free!

My friend, tear down your walls! And while you are doing your work of tearing down your walls, God will be doing His work of filling your heart with compassion and love for the lost. God will give you the desire to share Jesus with a lost and hurting world.

Remember, sharing the good news is all about Jesus. You love Jesus—I know you do! Oh, think about all He has done for you. How He has saved you from your sin. How He has turned your life around. How He has given you hope.

I received Jesus as my Savior when I was seven years old, and I shared Jesus with others the very next day. My fire and desire to tell others of Jesus has never weakened or left me. In the same way, Jesus can keep your heart full of your first love for Him.

Keep your eyes on Jesus and your heart pure. Jesus will keep you full of Himself. Then sharing Him with others will become the most natural thing in the world for you. Your love for Him will become so full and overflowing that you could not keep it to yourself if you tried.

∾∾∾

QUESTIONS TO CONSIDER

- Which temperature term describes your passion to share Jesus—*white hot, lukewarm,* or *stone cold*? Why is that?

- What external walls are preventing you from sharing Jesus? What internal walls?

- How can you tear down your walls?

3

THE HOLY SPIRIT IN CONTROL

Since we live by the Spirit, let us keep in step with the Spirit.

—Galatians 5:25 (NIV)

When I was growing up in Louisiana, still in my elementary school years, my family had a cotton farm. One of my chores was to carry buckets of water to the cotton choppers and cotton pickers at the far end of the field—a distance of almost a mile. You might think that would be a straightforward enough task, but God had surprising plans for it.

As I would carry the buckets of water, the Spirit of God would speak to me. He would say things like "I want you to go twenty steps straight ahead, then turn right and go fourteen steps, and then turn left again. After that, I want you to spin around three times and then go right."

Remember, this was the American South in the summertime. I was hot and tired. I just wanted to walk straight to the farm workers and give them their water. But I knew I had to do what the Spirit told me. It made for a long and complicated way to get across the field!

One day my dad found me on the other side of the cotton field from where I was expected to be. He asked, "What are you doing here?"

I told him that the Lord had instructed me to go there.

Then my dad (who wasn't walking in the Spirit yet) started chewing me out. In no uncertain terms, he told me where to go and what to do.

I went away, crying. What was I supposed to do? Was I supposed to obey God or my dad?

The Lord said to me, "It's all right. One day you'll be gone from here. You do what I'm telling you to do."

What I didn't understand then was that God was teaching me to listen to His voice. He was training me to follow His directions in every detail. In years to come, this training would come into play over and over again as I traveled the world and had to make decisions about which nation to go to next and who to speak with along the way.

Time and again, I lay out a map on the floor and pray over it, and Jesus will tell me which nation to go to, which road to take, the date on which to go, and the date on which to come back. Often I am led in almost every detail of the trip, even if it is to be a journey of many months. I stick to the plan God has given me and am confident that His covering is with me as I follow the way Jesus has shown me.

THE POWER IN OUR SHARING

We should never make the mistake of thinking that our sharing of Jesus is our own project. No, it is meant to be something that is directed by the Spirit and carried out under His control. Should we try to handle it on our own, we will have little if any success. In ourselves, we have no ability to bring about change in a person's heart; the power in our sharing comes from the Spirit working through us.

Jesus said, "When He, the Spirit of truth, has come, ... He will glorify Me" (John 16:13-14). And the Spirit glorifies Jesus (at least in part) by convicting people of their sin and drawing them to the Savior. Our part is simply to offer invitations for people to come to Jesus. It's not our convincing that does the work; it's the power of the Spirit.

Shortly before His ascension to heaven, Jesus promised His disciples, "You shall receive power when the Holy Spirit has come upon you" (Acts 1:8). And that's just what happened. On the Day of Pentecost, "when they had prayed, the place where they were assembled together was shaken; and they were all filled with the Holy Spirit, and they spoke the word of God with boldness. And with great power the apostles gave witness to the resurrection of the Lord Jesus" (Acts 4:31, 33).

There were 120 men and women who were praying in the upper room that day, 120 men and women who were filled with the Holy Spirit, 120 men and women who went out to tell the wonderful works of God. And three thousand people were saved. That's an average of twenty-five converts per witness on the Day of Pentecost.

That's what it's all about!

When we pray, God starts filling us with His Spirit, empowering us, and anointing the words we use in sharing Jesus with others. And the people we meet are never the same again.

SPECIFIC SPIRIT LEADING

Sometimes the Holy Spirit gets minutely involved in directing the witnesses of Jesus. He may give specific instructions, pushing us to do something or forbidding us to do something else, just as He did with several figures in the early history of the church.

~

Sometimes the Holy Spirit gets minutely involved in directing the witnesses of Jesus.

~

The apostle Philip had been carrying out a fruitful ministry in Samaria when he was told to go someplace else. "An angel of the Lord spoke to Philip, saying, 'Arise and go toward the south along the road which goes down from Jerusalem to Gaza' " (Acts 8:26). Philip obeyed. And when he got to his destination, he received more specific instructions: "Then the Spirit said unto Philip, Go near, and join thyself to this chariot" (Acts 8:29, KJV).

The Ethiopian eunuch (official) to whom the Spirit directed Philip was apparently part of a large caravan heading south. There may have been hundreds of chariots, horses, wagons, and the like traveling together. But God told Philip specifically who he was supposed to speak with. When the Spirit said, "Join thyself to this chariot," the Greek word translated "join thyself" means "glue." So, in effect, the Spirit said to Philip, "Go and glue yourself to that particular chariot." (It's always good to glue ourselves to the will of God!)

The Ethiopian was spiritually ready, and when Philip explained to Him about Jesus as the Messiah, the Ethiopian eagerly accepted Him and was baptized on the spot. "When they came up out of the water, the Spirit of the Lord caught Philip away, so that the eunuch saw him no more; and he went on his way rejoicing" (Acts 8:39). The Spirit had control over this encounter from beginning to end.

But Philip was by no means the only person whom the Spirit instructed back in those days.

On the important occasion when Peter learned that God accepts Gentiles as well as Jews who trust in Jesus, the Spirit of God arranged a meeting with Cornelius. The Spirit told Peter, "Behold, three men are seeking you. Arise therefore, go down and go with them" (Acts 10:19-20). The Spirit's instructions could not have been much clearer or more specific than that.

Then Paul, on one of his missionary journeys, was twice prevented by the Holy Spirit from going where he had planned. "When [Paul and Silas] had gone through Phrygia and the region of Galatia, they were forbidden by the Holy Spirit to preach the word in Asia. After they had come to Mysia, they tried to go into Bithynia, but the Spirit did not permit them" (Acts 16:6-7). The Holy Spirit used a vision to show Paul that he should go to Macedonia instead.

Was Paul trying to go to Asia or Bithynia on a vacation or a business trip? No, he was going to preach. There was nothing inherently wrong with his intentions. But the Spirit of God said no. He had other plans for Paul in Macedonia at that time.

At times, the Holy Spirit was specific in directing Jesus followers during New Testament times. The same is true today.

THE MAN IN THE WINDOW

Late one night in 1968, I was in Los Angeles, California, and another evangelist, Leo Humphrey, was in a car with me. I was driving and was about to head down to the Sunset Strip, when suddenly the Lord gave me a vision. In my mind, I clearly saw the image of a man sitting by a second-floor window with a light shining over his shoulder. The Lord said, "That man's ready to be saved. I want to lead you to him."

I turned to my companion and said, "Leo, would you drive?"

"Where are we going?"

"Just drive." Then I began giving directions. "Go out of here and turn left up there." A little later I'd say, "Take that next street to the right." As we traveled, I could feel that we were getting nearer and nearer to where God wanted us to go.

We kept turning. Then I said, "Now, tell me when you see a second-floor window open with a man visible in it. You can just see the top of his head and a light shining over his shoulder."

After a little while, Leo slammed on the brakes and started crying. He said, "There he is."

We got out of the car and went up to the taxi dispatcher's office where the man was sitting. Even though it was two o'clock in the morning at the time, we knocked on the door and the man inside said, "Come in."

I explained, "I've come to tell you how to receive Jesus."

A Bible was lying open before him. He said, "I've been studying the Bible. I don't know how to be saved. I want to be." And we led him to Jesus.

SPAIN INSTEAD

Many times, when carrying the cross around the world, I have felt God directing me to one place instead of to another.

In 1972 I was in Europe, carrying the cross, and from Paris I planned to head into Germany. But on the morning after I'd spent the night in Paris, when I picked up the cross and started to walk, I felt the Spirit speaking to me. He said, "Don't take another step. That's not the way."

What a strange feeling! I had no peace about going to Germany now. It was like there was a wall in front of me. So I thought, *Well, then, I'll head up to northern Europe. I'll go to Amsterdam.*

Again, no peace, only a wall in my mind. Apparently I was not supposed to go to Holland anymore than to Germany.

At last I prayed, "Lord, where do You want me to go? Do You want me to go to Spain?" Now I felt a release in my spirit. I turned south and headed for Spain that very moment.

There was nothing bad about ministering in Germany or Holland; eventually I made it to both countries. But at that moment, God wanted me somewhere else. And in fact, my ministry in Spain was one of the most glorious (though difficult) of any during my long cross walk around the world.

Francisco Franco was still in charge of the nation, and freedoms—including the freedoms to worship and assemble—were limited. When I got to Spain, I was arrested within the first mile. I was released before long, but then, when I made it to Madrid and began speaking in the Plaza Mayor to tens of thousands of people, the civil guard beat me and several others in the crowd. But none of it kept me from carrying the cross and sharing about Jesus. It was the beginning of a nationwide revival in Spain.

And it all began with God saying, "Go *there*," and me obeying.

HOW WE HEAR THE SPIRIT SPEAK

After I was saved at age seven, I used to love to climb up in the old pin oak tree in the front yard of our farmhouse. I'd find a comfortable branch to perch on, and I'd pray all night.

This pleased my mother, but it worried her too. She would set her alarm clock, and every hour on the hour, she would holler out the window, "Son, are you okay?"

"Yes, Mama, I'm okay."

"Don't fall asleep and fall out of that tree."

"No, ma'am."

Up in that tree, under the night sky, I had a great time with God all night. I would visit with Him, and He would visit with me. And many nights since then, in far-flung corners of the earth, I have had the same sort of experience.

In 1988 I flew the cross into Angola, which was in the midst of civil war at the time, and I was held hostage for a week in an old camp before being permitted to carry the cross. Every night, I would look up at the sky and visit with God.

One night in 1977, in the Golan Heights, I got lost between the Israeli army and the Syrians. So I had to spend the night lying on a bus stop board that people had sat on while waiting for the bus. (The board was the only part of the bus stop that was still standing; the bus stop had been blown up during the fighting.) I spent the night hours praying intimately with the Father.

Two years later, near the end of my time carrying the cross through the Darién jungle (partly in Panama, partly in Colombia), I emerged at a small village in Colombia. The only place I could find to spend the night was on some boards that I laid over a pigpen—I called it "Pig Hilton." The pigs kept grunting and rooting about all night, keeping me awake despite my aching and my exhaustion. But God was there, and I had a wonderful night with Him.

Oh, I pray that I will never lose what I found up in that old pin oak tree when I was a child! I have a friendship, a love relationship with God in which I constantly talk to Him and He talks to me.

It is out of this kind of close relationship, which we cultivate with God every day, that we hear the Spirit give us our directions.

~

*I have a friendship, a love relationship
with God in which I constantly talk
to Him and He talks to me.*

~

But someone might ask: "How can we know that we are really hearing the voice of God?" There is no simple answer to this question, but let me give you a few test questions to ask yourself. *Does what you are hearing line up with the Word of God?* The Holy Spirit will never tell us to do anything that contradicts Scripture. *Does it sound like Jesus?*

The more we know Him, the easier it is to tell if something is consistent with His ways. *Does it produce the fruit of the Spirit—love, joy, peace, longsuffering, kindness, goodness, faithfulness, gentleness, self-control?* When it does, it must be right. (For articles on knowing the will of God and doing it, go to www.blessitt.com/weekly/archive.html.)

YES OR NO

Here's another question that might be in somebody's mind: "If I don't hear a specific leading from the Holy Spirit, should I do nothing?" Answer: certainly not.

Jesus has already given us our marching orders: "Go ... and make disciples of all the nations, baptizing them in the name of the Father and of the Son and of the Holy Spirit, teaching them to observe all things that I have commanded you" (Matthew 28:19-20). We should assume, based on this, that we should be sharing Jesus every opportunity we get. Should the Holy Spirit want to fine-tune our sharing from time to time by telling us, "Go here" or "Go there," that's great. But we should never *not* share Jesus unless the Spirit specifically tells us so.

I've found there are two kinds of Jesus followers. The first are those who never share Jesus unless they receive some kind of revelation. These almost never lead people to the Lord. The second are those who speak to everybody they can unless the Lord says not to do it. It is these who are helping the lost people of the world find the Jesus they love so much.

Now, having said that we should not be stymied when we don't get a specific leading from the Spirit, let me hasten to repeat that sometimes we *will* get that kind of specific leading. Indeed, we should be expecting it and be listening for it at all times. Sound unlikely to you?

Assuming you are a follower of Jesus, I guarantee you that someday the Spirit of God will speak to you. You will be sitting in a restaurant and see a patron at another table, and you will know that God wants you to share Jesus with that person. You will be driving home and come upon a disabled car stopped by the side of the road, and you will sense a prompting to stop and help. You will be shopping and notice a woman who is upset because her kids are crying, and you will want to say, "God bless you."

There is no question that the Spirit will speak to us. The question is, how will we respond?

Let's consider what might happen should we decide to ignore the Spirit's guidance. In Scripture, that's called "quenching" the Holy Spirit (1 Thessalonians 5:19). The Greek word for "quench" was used to refer to blowing out a light. It doesn't take much to blow out a light, does it? Just so easily can we say no to the Spirit's leading.

When we reject the Spirit's leading like that, the Bible tells us, we "grieve the Holy Spirit of God" (Ephesians 4:30). The Holy Spirit is a person, just like Jesus is and just like the Father is. And since the Spirit is a person, we cause Him pain when we reject or suppress what He tells us to do.

But ignoring guidance from the Spirit has an impact not only upon Him but upon us as well. The Bible warns us,

Today, if you will hear His voice,
Do not harden your hearts. (Hebrews 4:7)

Ignoring the Spirit hardens our hearts the way manual labor gives our hands calluses. And so it becomes that much harder to obey the Spirit the next time.

When we say yes to the Spirit, on the other hand, our hearts are softened. Our ears become better attuned to hearing the Spirit's voice, and it becomes easier for us to say yes the next time. We go from obedience to obedience in the marvelous adventure of following the Spirit's leading.

സസസ

QUESTIONS TO CONSIDER

- Is there spiritual power in your sharing of Jesus? Why or why not?

- What changes could you make in your relationship with God so that you will be better prepared to hear the Spirit when He speaks?

- What, if anything, might the Spirit be telling you to do right now?

4

POWER
THROUGH
PRAYER

*[People] always ought to pray and not lose
heart.*

—Luke 18:1

My father came back from World War II with
his heart far from the Lord and with a serious
drinking problem. I was four years old at the
time. My first memory of my dad, in fact, is of him drinking in a bar while I watched the bubbles go around and
around on the jukebox.

My next memory is of my mother praying for Dad. In
fact, every night when Dad was out drinking, Mom would
stay up and pray for him to come home and for him to
give his heart to the Lord. I often joined her in praying
during the night.

One night, when I was thirteen, Dad staggered into the
house drunk. As I had done before on such occasions, I
said to him, "Dad, it's time to give your heart to Jesus." He
had always resisted my appeals before, but for some rea-

son, this night was different. He fell on his knees beside the couch, and my family gathered around Dad and prayed with him as he began a new life of following Jesus.

After all the prayers and constant witness, my father committed his life to Jesus and was a changed man the rest of his life, becoming a beautiful follower of Jesus.

PRAYING PERSISTENTLY

What are we supposed to do about the lost people in the world? After all, there are so many of them. Even Jesus said, "The harvest truly is plentiful." We are to *pray*. "Pray the Lord of the harvest to send out laborers into His harvest" (Matthew 9:37-38).

That statement by Jesus tells us what to pray for, and it isn't for God to save somebody. We already know that "the Lord is … not willing that any should perish but that all should come to repentance" (2 Peter 3:9). So we don't have to plead with Him to save someone; that is already the desire of His heart. Instead, we are to pray for laborers—for God to inspire His people to obey His command and share Jesus with the lost. And we ourselves are to be a part of the answer to that prayer.

The Greek word for "pray" in Matthew 9:38 means "to beg." So, in other words, we are to beg and plead with the Lord to send forth laborers. That's persistent, passionate prayer that Jesus is calling for.

Nearly all the time, when I sign my name to a letter or e-mail message, I add the verse reference Luke 18:1. That verse says, "[People] always ought to pray and not lose heart." We need reminders to pray constantly, without growing weary. Our sharing about Jesus, as well as every other aspect of our life, should be saturated in prayer.

The apostle Paul made the same point in different words, saying we are to "pray without ceasing" (1 Thessalonians 5:17). What does that mean? How can we be in prayer every moment, since after all we've got other things to do in life? Let me give you an illustration.

Have you ever been on a long car trip with somebody close to you, maybe a friend or your spouse? I bet you have. And I bet there were times on that trip when one of you pointed out a beautiful scene. "Look at that mountain!" You talked about the magnificent mountain for a bit, and then the conversation lapsed. A little while later, you talked about something else.

In a situation like that, when the other person says, "Look at that mountain!" you don't say, "Yeah, it's beautiful. Well, goodbye," do you? No, on a lengthy trip you might stop talking from time to time, but the conversation picks up again with ease. It's really just one long conversation you're having, with breaks.

It's the same way with constant prayer. Praying without ceasing is never saying goodbye to God. It is never saying amen. It is speaking to Him whenever we have something to say, big or little. And it is being open for Him to speak to us at any time, day or night. We are constantly aware of the unchanging presence of Jesus.

When we're praying this way, we never faint. Instead, we're strengthened. We go from blessing to blessing, from strength to strength. Jesus wants us to live in His power and share about Him in His power and in His presence.

PRAYING FOR FAVOR

When it comes to sharing about Jesus, what should we pray for? One thing is favor. When we notice someone who appears downcast in a store and we want to offer to pray with this person, we should first ask God to give us favor with this person so that our offer will be well received. When we go door to door sharing Jesus alongside a team from our church, we should pray that whoever opens the door will look upon us favorably.

We don't pray for favor so that we will be liked. No. It's not about us; it's about Jesus. Maybe we're sweaty and tongue-tied, and we don't present a very appealing image of ourselves. Regardless, we want to find favor so that the other person has an interest in the Savior we are introducing him or her to.

We find favor with people when we have first found favor with God. Why? Because people can tell when we have a vital connection with God and that is always appealing.

Having favor with God doesn't mean we are perfect, but it does mean that God has forgiven us through His Son and that He is pleased with our attempts at being faithful to follow Him. God answers the prayers of those who have found favor with Him, because they pray according to His will.

The Bible tells us of several people who found favor with God, including Samuel the priest and judge (1 Samuel 2:26). Samuel had one of the closest walks with God recorded in Scripture, and God answered his prayers. The Bible tells us, "The LORD was with him and let none of his words fall to the ground" (3:19). How would you like to have a prayer life like that?

God gave Joseph favor even in prison (Genesis 39:21), and Joseph then rose to be the second in command of Egypt. In this way, Joseph became the one God used to save the children of Israel from starving.

But favor with God is not for men only. A young woman named Mary from Nazareth heard from an angel, "You have found favor with God" (Luke 1:30). She was given the great honor of bearing the Son of God.

But the greatest example of favor is Jesus. We are told that, as a child, "Jesus increased in wisdom and stature, and in favor with God and men" (Luke 2:52). God opened the way for Jesus to serve Him, and the Father heard and answered Jesus' every prayer.

We need to pray for God to have favor upon us and to give us favor with others so that they will respond to our sharing of Jesus.

PRAYING FOR THE ENEMY TO BE FRUSTRATED

Many times, I have been around followers of Jesus who, in a spiritual warfare situation, will call out, "I rebuke you, Satan!" This makes me cringe. It's not that I have any problem with someone taking the fight to our enemy. Rather, it's because the Scriptures tell us that we are not supposed to rebuke the enemy ourselves but instead are supposed to say, "The Lord rebuke you!" (Jude 9).

That's what I say as I carry the cross around the world. Not necessarily out loud, but in my spirit, I say,

"The Lord rebuke you, devil. This is God's territory." There is no part of the earth's surface where God cannot take control and force out the influence of our spiritual enemy, and that's what I am calling for Him to do. I couldn't do it on my own.

The biblical word for "rebuke" means "to forbid." So when we say to the enemy, "The Lord rebuke you," we are really saying, "The Lord forbid you from having your way." We are calling on God to block the schemes of the enemy.

There is power in asking God to rebuke the works of the devil.

As I have carried the cross in certain places in the world, it has aroused hatred in many. I've had people come at me with nails and a hammer, intending to nail me to the cross. I've had guns stuck to my head. I've heard every kind of threat issued against me. But I'm still here. How? Not by taking action myself but by saying to the Lord, "You take care of it."

Given that we are not supposed to rebuke our spiritual enemy, what *are* we supposed to do? We are to bind and loose. Jesus promised, "I will give you the keys of the kingdom of heaven, and whatever you bind on earth will be bound in heaven, and whatever you loose on earth will be loosed in heaven" (Matthew 16:19). When I'm walking, therefore, I pray, "Lord, bind every work of Satan. Loose Your Holy Spirit."

When you are sharing Jesus with someone who seems bound and is not free to respond, pray, "Lord, I ask that this blindness will be gone. Loose your Holy Spirit in his life. Bind the evil spirits and loose Your Holy Spirit."

~

*I'm praying for God's work to be done in
their lives and for Him to frustrate the
work of the enemy.*

~

Often, when I meet people on the road, I'll shake their
hand and grin at them. What they don't know is that I'm
also praying at the same time. I'm praying for God's
work to be done in their lives and for Him to frustrate the
work of the enemy.

Most people don't know much about my prayer life, but
I'm praying every day, every moment on the roads. And as
I take each step, I'm saying the name of Jesus: "Jesus,
Jesus, Jesus ..." And as I drive, I say His name to the tele-
phone poles and to the white lines: "Jesus, Jesus, Jesus
..." Many days, I say His name thousands of times. Why?
Because He is loosing His Spirit; He is opening the way.

That's what we are to do as we go out into the world
to share Jesus. Pray, pray, pray.

FASTING WITH PRAYER

One day, when Jesus' disciples failed to cast out a
demon, they asked the Lord what had gone wrong. He
told them, "This kind does not go out except by prayer
and fasting" (Matthew 17:21). In other words, there are
times when prayer alone is not enough; we also need to
fast in order to bring to bear extra spiritual power. To
shake the hold of the enemy on unbelievers, many times
we need to fast *and* pray.

Fasting—or voluntarily going without eating food for a period of time—is a theme that runs throughout the Scriptures. Moses fasted when he received the Ten Commandments (Exodus 34:28). Jesus fasted after His baptism (Matthew 4:2). The leaders of the church fasted before sending out their first missionaries (Acts 13:2-3). And this is just the start of the examples of great men and women of the Bible who fasted at important junctures of their lives.

Jesus said to His followers, "When you fast ..." (Matthew 6:16-17), implying that they *would* fast. And in fact, down through the ages, followers of Jesus have fasted. Historical records show that just about every great follower of Jesus in history fasted at crucial times in his or her life.

When I was ministering in Hollywood in 1969, certain community leaders kicked me out of our building on Sunset Strip. They said we were out of taste with the community. (Of course, the Whiskey-a-Go-Go was next door, and the topless nightclub Sneaky Pete's was directly below us—these were apparently fine for the community's taste.) When I was evicted, I moved the cross down from our meeting space, chained myself to it, and fasted with only water for twenty-eight days until the people on Sunset Strip got me another building.

During this time of fasting, revival broke out. Many people were saved. That area had previously had one of the highest crime rates around, but before long, the crime rate had dropped to almost nothing. That street was totally changed.

When we want to see a breakthrough with a stubborn person who won't receive Christ, we should pray and fast. There's no guarantee that our fasting will result in a decision for Christ, but I have seen it happen again and again. I can't explain how it works, but somehow our fasting makes a difference in the spirit world.

You can fast for just one meal or for a week or longer. You can drink water only or you can drink juice during your fast. And at some point in your fast, should you feel that you need to stop it before reaching your original goal, don't feel like a failure. Do whatever God leads you to do.

It's not the *when* or *how* of your fasting that I am concerned about. Instead, I am concerned that the followers of Jesus in greater numbers take up this tool to bring extra power to their sharing of Jesus. Praying and fasting, together, are a powerful combination that can knock down spiritual strongholds that had appeared invulnerable.

PRAYER AND ORDINARY PEOPLE

Should sharing Jesus be reduced to mere technique, then no matter how great that technique was, it would be powerless and largely ineffective. Rather, sharing Jesus ought to be a *spiritual* activity. It should be one that is led by the Spirit (as we have already seen) and one that is bathed in prayer and backed up with fasting. Someone who is awkward in sharing Jesus, but who has prayed and labored with the Lord over the salvation of others, is going to be used by God far more effectively than is someone who is merely following a plan.

You see, it is men and women like us—ordinary people—who God uses to bring others in His kingdom. He does it by pouring Himself into a heart that's willing to have Him there. Prayer and fasting give us power beyond ourselves. They give us divine power.

Let's put our lives, our prayers, and our hearts into the service of God. Let's pray for Him to release favor in our witness, to bring the power of the Holy Spirit into our lives, and to turn people from the blindness of Satan to the light of Christ. As we give ourselves, He will move through us.

~ ~ ~

QUESTIONS TO CONSIDER

• What evidence do you have that when you share Jesus it is a spiritual activity and not just a technique?

• What aspects of your sharing do you feel that you should be praying about right now?

• Do you sense that the Lord is calling you to fast? If so, with what purpose in mind?

5

THE GLORY OF THE LORD IN YOU

The LORD said: ... "Truly, as I live, all the earth shall be filled with the glory of the LORD."

—Numbers 14:20-21

In 1979 I was in Iquitos, Peru, with my daughter Gina and my friend Mike Ooten, preparing to take the cross down the Amazon River by boat. One night, as usual, I was reading the Scriptures before going to bed, when suddenly I was filled with a desire for God to reveal His thoughts to me. I prayed, "Lord, if there is anything You'd like to say tonight, You can speak whatever is in Your heart and in Your mind, and I will do it for Your glory." Then, about two o'clock in the morning, I fell asleep.

An hour later I woke up and began to see a vision that was like nothing else I've ever seen, either before or since. It was as if a window opened up and I could see far beyond the room I was lying in, beyond the earth, and even beyond outer space. Past all the galaxies, I could see a tiny glowing speck in the far distance. Moment by moment, the speck was growing in size as it came closer to the earth. Soon I could see that it looked like a fiery stream made up of rolling, swirling light in bright colors—red, gold, and orange. Strangely, the swirling was not moving from top to bottom, like ocean waves curling over, but instead was moving from the bottom to the top.

I tried to cry out, but I was speechless. I could not move. The mighty wind of the golden glow was sweeping toward the earth, and all I could do was to try to take it in. As it drew closer, I could see that there were a host of people and angels just beyond the golden swirl. The brightness behind the fire was blinding—silver and ultra-white.

Then words appeared before my eyes: "Arthur, proclaim that the glory of the coming of the Lord is at hand." Those words stayed before my eyes for the entire rest of the vision. I knew now what I was seeing: it was a vision of the coming of the glory of the Lord.

As I watched, the divine glory swept over the earth, leaving it white and sparkling clean. Then it came into my room and swept over me, enveloping me in its glow. Again and again, it would recede and return. From the bottom of my feet to the top of my head, the glory swept over me like waves.

In the midst of all this, I evidently groaned out loud, because I woke up Gina and Mike, who were sleeping nearby. Gina—fifteen years old at the time—said, "Daddy's having a stroke."

I could not speak for a while, but then I managed to say, "Can't you see the glory of the Lord? Look! Look!" But they could not see what I was seeing.

Mike reassured Gina: "Arthur is with the Lord."

I sat on the floor and prayed, "Lord, I don't need a vision. I love You. I will follow You. I don't want to get off preaching Jesus into something else." I was concerned because it sounded to me as if God was calling me to a ministry of prophecy instead of to evangelism.

But the Lord interrupted me and said, "Fear not. Receive what I am giving you. Release yourself to Me."

All strength left my body and I lay on the floor as one dead for four hours, until eight o'clock in the morning. I cannot tell all I saw, but I continued to see and experience the glory of the coming of the Lord. Oh, how indescribably wonderful it was!

At one point the Lord let me experience the horror—the awful horror—of the first moment when an unsaved person dies and realizes he has missed the glory of the coming of the Lord, with everything lost for all eternity. Oh, what pain in my mind, body, and soul! I burst into tears. Agony gripped me.

Then the beauty and the glory of the coming of the Lord appeared before me again, and I thrilled in every part of my being.

Finally the Lord spoke again: "I have chosen you, Arthur, to proclaim that the glory of the coming of the Lord is at hand."

Mike and Gina had sat for hours watching over me. Now, as the vision receded, I motioned for a glass of water, and after drinking it, I could speak. Briefly, I explained to the two what I had been through. My body was exhausted as I fell back into bed and slipped into a deep sleep, resting in the glory of the Lord.

FROM GLORY TO GLORY

You may never experience a vision anything like the one I had in Peru. And that's just fine; God has other things for you. But trust me when I say this: *any* faithful follower of Jesus can experience the glory of the Lord.

Moses, the great leader of the Hebrews, ascended Mount Sinai to receive the Ten Commandments. There the Lord met him in a cloud with lightning forking from it. Afterward, "his face shone while he talked with Him" (Exodus 34:29). The radiance so disturbed others that Moses temporarily had to wear a veil over his face.

But Moses wasn't the only one to see the glory of the Lord in that day. The entire nation of Israel saw God's glory hovering over the tabernacle (their worship tent). By day, this glory appeared in the form of a pillar of cloud, while at night it appeared as a pillar of fire. When the cloud moved, the nation would advance; when the cloud stayed put, the people would travel nowhere.

Today the tabernacle—or temple—of God is the believer (1 Corinthians 3:16-17). By His Spirit, He dwells within those who are followers of His Son. And thus, in our own way, we are to live under the cloud of glory and in the fire of the Holy Spirit.

How do we get this glory inside us? It's a gift from Jesus. He gives us *His* glory.

One day, like a latter-day Moses, Jesus took some of His disciples up a mountain. There Jesus "was transfigured before them. His face shone like the sun, and His clothes became as white as the light" (Matthew 17:2). This was Jesus' true nature of glory shining forth. Peter's offer to build a "tabernacle," or booth, for Jesus to stay in made no sense, because Jesus Himself was a tabernacle containing the glory of God.

◯

How do we get this glory inside us? It's a gift from Jesus. He gives us His glory.

◯

Later, shortly before His crucifixion, Jesus prayed to the Father in the presence of His disciples, "The glory which You gave Me I have given them" (John 17:22). In other words, the glory of God is within us because Jesus has put it there. We have Jesus' glory, not because we are deserving of it, but because God is merciful and gracious to pour out His Spirit.

This glory builds up in us as we live for Jesus. The apostle Paul declared, "We all, with unveiled face, beholding as in a mirror the glory of the Lord, are being transformed into the same image from glory to glory, just as by the Spirit of the Lord" (2 Corinthians 3:18). Paul was saying that, as we focus on God, it is like looking in a mirror and seeing, not an image of ourselves, but the image of God. And the more we look at it, the more we become like the image we see. The Spirit of God changes us and fills us with the presence of God until we start looking like Jesus. Isn't that marvelous?

One time, when I was carrying the cross in Switzerland, a man rushed up to me and said in broken English, "You look like that cross."

Bemused, I replied, "Well, thank you so much, friend."

As I traveled down the road, I thought, *Man that was weird. He thought I looked like the cross.* I leaned the cross against a post and stared at it. I had been using that cross for years, and it was beat up and battered. I didn't know that I looked that rough.

All of a sudden it came to me. Yes! I want to look like the cross. I want to look like my Lord. I pray that my mannerisms, my thoughts, my actions—everything about me—will remind people of Jesus.

After all, where is the glory of God? It is "in the face of Jesus" (2 Corinthians 4:6). So if we want to see the glory of God, we must get to know Jesus. As we let Him fill our lives, we are filled with the glory of the Lord.

GLORY IN OUR SHARING

Now, what does all this have to do with sharing Jesus? I'll tell you. As we share Jesus, we can know that the glory of God is within us and we can spread it to others so that they are drawn by it to God. This is an insight that can revolutionize our sharing.

Since the Lord Jesus has saved us, He lives in us. And now, as we speak His name, as we proclaim His presence, the glory of God is there. People know it. They sense it. They see it in our eyes and in our countenance. And this makes it much easier for people to come to Jesus.

Imagine you are talking with a teenage boy and he introduces you to five girls, one of whom is his sweetheart. You can tell which one is his girl, can't you? He says, "Here are Martha and Amy and Sue and Alice and *Jane*." When he refers to Jane, he lights up. You can tell he's in love with her.

~

Everywhere you proclaim Jesus, that's where the glory of God is.

~

In the same way, people can tell when someone is sharing Jesus in the glory of the Holy Spirit. When we mention the name of Jesus, others can tell we are in love with Him. We don't say "Jesus" in the same way we say "Hector" or some other name. Our love for Him comes through. That's the glory of God in our conversation, our life, and our witness.

Everywhere you proclaim Jesus, that's where the glory of God is. Indeed, it is not just when we proclaim Jesus that we can know the glory; the glory can and should be a part of everything we do. "Whether you eat or drink, or whatever you do, do all to the glory of God" (1 Corinthians 10:31). Even the simplest thing may be anointed by God, and then everything becomes a blessing and a joy.

As a follower of Jesus, you already have the glory of God inside you. Just let it come out. Live in the awareness of God's glory. Cultivate that glory in you by obeying and worshiping and speaking with Jesus. And then let it shine forth from you like light through a sparkling-clear window. People will see it, and they will feel that they *have* to have what you have inside yourself: the glory of the Lord.

Back in Peru, when I was receiving the vision of God's glory, I was mistaken about one thing. I was worried that God was calling me to a different ministry, leading me away from evangelism and into prophecy. And honestly, I have never really been sure about a lot of the prophetic interpretations of the Bible. I've always been a simple sharer of Jesus.

In fact, I told the Lord that day in Peru, "I'm not able. I'm just a road man, with dirty blue jeans and a cross. You have big TV preachers, big crusade evangelists, large organizations." I thought He should tap someone else to deliver His prophetic message.

But God wasn't calling me to a different ministry, leading me away from evangelism and into prophecy. Now, I think He wanted me to be more intentional about preaching the coming of the glory of the Lord to people. But primarily, He wanted me to start consciously doing my sharing in the glory of the Lord. It was a qualitative difference in what I was already about.

That's a qualitative difference you can have, too, as you share Jesus with those who need to know Him.

IN ALL THE EARTH

Come to think of it, maybe I will get prophetic for a minute. I want to remind you of something God promised: "Truly, as I live, all the earth shall be filled with the glory of the LORD" (Numbers 14:21).

Many of us think this is referring to some dramatic time in history that is still to come, some end-times occurrence. Well, I'm here to tell you that it's happening right now. The whole earth is even now being filled with the glory of the Lord. As we proclaim Jesus in all the earth, the glory of God is covering every square mile. That's a marvelous fulfillment of prophecy that each of us has a part in.

Every time we proclaim Jesus in our neighborhood or wherever else we are, we are spreading the glory of the Lord there. That's why it's so important that every follower of Jesus respond to His call to go into the world with His message— so that, by all of us working together, we can spread God's glory everywhere. He deserves to be glorified in every creature He has made.

Worried that you cannot contribute to such a lofty goal? Remember this, my fellow servant of Jesus. God has not sent you out empty-handed. God's Spirit and His glory are with you. And as you are faithful to Him, He *will* manifest His glory within you.

So the next time you're waiting at the bus stop or in line at your bank, don't think it is just a ho-hum situation with no particular meaning. Think *Jesus is here at this bus stop with me, here at this bank with me. The glory of God is here. May it fill me to the brim and overflow so that these people next to me can sense it.* Then speak.

I'll say it one more time. Let the glory that Jesus has given you be manifest in your life and your witness. Don't quench the glory of God—oh, no! Instead, let it flow like a mighty stream of flame throughout all the world!

∾∾∾

QUESTIONS TO CONSIDER

- What evidence do you have that the glory of God is inside you?

- How can you let the glory of God shine forth from your countenance more plainly?

PART 2
THE CONVERSATION

6

TELLING YOUR STORY

*Let the redeemed of the Lord say so,
whom He has redeemed from the hand of
the enemy.*

—Psalm 107:2

When I was seven, in 1947, my family moved to a small farm near Oak Grove, Louisiana. One Sunday our pastor, Brother Dewey Mercer, announced that a brush-arbor revival was going to break out the following week. An evangelist from Texas would be the preacher. Something in me stirred. I was only seven, but I knew I was a sinner. "All have sinned," I remembered from Romans 5:12 (KJV).

We arrived for the first night of the revival to find a makeshift church set up in the parking lot. We sat under a roof of boards, tree limbs, and brush held in place by a dozen slim poles, each topped by a naked light bulb. The preaching came fast and forceful, ending with a call from the evangelist for sinners to step to the pulpit and be saved.

I started to go forward, but my mother grabbed me by the shirt. "You're cutting up, son," she said.

She wouldn't let me go. And I couldn't blame her. I had wiggled all through the service, but it was the wiggling of impatience and excitement rather than that of boredom or inattention. No one had ever been more anxious to get up and be counted for Christ, but I couldn't convince my mother to let me.

On the ride home I asked Mom, "Why wouldn't you let me go up to the front with the others?"

"Why did you want to go?"

"I wanted to be saved!"

"We'll be back tomorrow night, and the same fellow will be preaching."

"But I want to be saved tonight!"

Dad, who had been unresponsive up till this point, suddenly screeched our truck to a halt in the middle of the road. He shifted into reverse, backed up, and wheeled toward the brush arbor. I knew that ribbon of road was leading me straight to Christ.

I had always loved Jesus and wanted to live for Him. But on this night, for the first time, I felt lost and separated from Jesus. I was aware of my need and immediately wanted Jesus in my life forever.

Brother Mercer and the evangelist were still in the parking lot when we returned. After Dad talked to them, the two preachers came over to me. "All you have to do, son, is ask Jesus into your heart," the evangelist said. "Accept Him as your Savior and know that He died on the cross for you. Then you can be saved, right here, right at this moment."

"I'm ready."

We knelt and I repeated each line of the brief prayer offered by the evangelist. "Dear God, I know I'm a sinner. I ask Jesus to come into my heart and live in my life forever. Make my home heaven. Thank You, Jesus."

My sin washed away, I went to sleep that night knowing that Jesus was my best friend and that He always would be. And He always has been.

That period of about an hour or so was the only time in my life when I have ever felt lost and separated from Jesus. I have had the privilege of living with Jesus all my life.

MAKING LIFE WITH JESUS PERSONAL

You have just read my testimony, my story of coming to Jesus. I started sharing it with others the very day after I accepted Christ. I told my friends and even my dad—who had not yet fully committed his life to Jesus—about how I had been changed by God.

I've been telling the same testimony ever since. You might not think that the testimony of a seven year old praying with an evangelist at church would have much of an impact. But that hasn't stopped me from sharing it with effect with all kinds of people, including gatherings of Hell's Angels and terrorists. Why? Because it's the truth; and the truth always has power.

～

It isn't the length of the story or your story-telling ability that matters most; it is your honesty about your experience with Jesus.

～

Let me strongly encourage you, when you are sharing Jesus with an unbeliever, to tell your own story of coming to Jesus. Sometimes you might go into considerable detail about coming to know Jesus and about your life with Him. Other times, you might be far less circumstantial. It isn't the length of the story or your storytelling ability that matters most; it is your honesty about your experience with Jesus.

Sometimes, in a brief encounter with an unbeliever, I have offered nothing more in the way of a testimony than words like "I have experienced Jesus, and you can too." And I have found that saying even as little as that can grab people's attention. For example, I have been sharing Jesus in Europe, where for many the Christian faith is just an archaic set of traditions, and when I say that I have a personal relationship with God Almighty, people will stop and say, "Really?!"

When I simply say that I talk with God in prayer, people of other religions are often amazed. Many Muslims, for example, believe that God quit speaking with people after Muhammad died. And many Jews connect the idea of talking with God only with the elders of their faith, such as Abraham and Moses. So the idea that I have a personal relationship with God and talk to Him brings them up short. They are ready to listen to what I have to share about Jesus.

Should you fail to share your personal testimony, unbelievers might think that what you are saying about Jesus is merely a philosophy or a theory. But you want them to know that following Jesus is *personal* and that it is *life changing*. You can do that by telling what following Him has meant to you.

Next to your testimony of who Jesus is (we'll be getting to that in the next chapter), the most powerful thing you can share with people is your own personal testimony of knowing Christ.

WE CANNOT BUT SPEAK

Offering a testimony about one's own experience with Jesus is not just good advice; it is a biblical pattern. Indeed, it seems that when people met Jesus during His time on earth, they couldn't stop talking about Him. The same should hold true for us when we have met Him, for our experience of Him is just as real even though it has not occurred face to face. "We also believe and therefore speak" (2 Corinthians 4:13).

The Gospels are full of stories about people encountering Jesus. Those are stories that were passed around for years until they were recorded by one or more of the Gospel writers. Clearly those events had a big impact on the people involved, and since then they have had a big impact on all of us who have heard or read them.

Several times the Gospels explicitly tell of people sharing with others about Jesus.

The woman whom Jesus met at a well in Samaria ran back to her village and started talking about Jesus with everyone she could find. What was the result? "Many of the Samaritans of that city believed in Him because of the word of the woman who testified, 'He told me all that I ever did'" (John 4:39).

On another occasion, after Jesus had healed a man who had been blind from birth, religious officials expressed their disdain for Jesus because they didn't know where He was from. The newly sighted man boldly stated, "Why, this is a marvelous thing, that you do not know where He is from; yet He has opened my eyes! Now we know that God does not hear sinners; but if anyone is a worshiper of God and does His will, He hears him. Since the world began it has been unheard of that anyone opened the eyes of one who was born blind. If this Man were not from God, He could do nothing" (John 9:30-33).

When Jesus cast demons out of a man in the region known as the Decapolis, the man wanted to go with Jesus. "However, Jesus did not permit him, but said to him, 'Go home to your friends, and tell them what great things the Lord has done for you, and how He has had compassion on you.' And he departed and began to proclaim in Decapolis all that Jesus had done for him; and all marveled" (Mark 5:19-20).

The book of Acts records the story of the conversion of Saul—later called Paul the apostle—no fewer than three times (Acts 9:1-19; 22:1-21; 26:1-23). Two of these are actually accounts of Paul himself sharing the story with others. At critical moments in his life (when on the verge of being mobbed in the temple and when standing trial before a national leader), he chose to recount his story of meeting Jesus on the road to Damascus.

When Peter and John were ordered to cease preaching about Jesus, they retorted, "We cannot but speak the things which we have seen and heard" (Acts 4:20). May that be our attitude, too!

TESTIFYING IS FOR EVERYONE

As we saw in the biblical examples, sharing with others about one's experience with Jesus is for everyone: new believers and mature believers, men and women, the educated and the uneducated, people who have led a relatively moral life and people who have been exceptionally sinful—everyone who has been saved through grace!

Sometimes people will say of a new believer, "Let him learn more about the faith and be discipled before we ask him to speak with anyone else about Jesus." No! Even a brand-new convert can give a testimony, just like the woman at the well, the newly sighted man, and the former demoniac.

Immediately after leading someone to Christ, I often will say something to this person like "Tell your friend here what you have just done" or "Go home right away and share with your husband what has happened to you." Often the new believer has so much enthusiasm that his or her testimony is powerful, even though the new believer may at this point know little about the Bible or about following Jesus.

The experience of sharing with others also solidifies in new believers the salvation that has occurred in their lives. These persons have now gone public with their experience. Others will be watching to see whether they follow through by sticking with Jesus and submitting to making changes in their lives.

New followers of Christ should always be encouraged to share about Jesus right from the start; they should never be disqualified from offering their testimony. On the other hand, people will sometimes try to disqualify themselves, saying, "I can't witness for Jesus. I've got so much sin in my life right now." Sadly, there is some truth to this.

The power of God doesn't work in a life of sin. When we are living in sin, we have His chastening upon us, not His anointing. Certainly God, in His goodness, might sometimes choose to use a testimony from someone who is living with sin. But my experience is that He will not consistently bless the testifying of a believer who is not striving to walk with Him.

~

To take up His cross and follow Him means to obey Him by sharing God's love in a needy world.

~

The solution to all this is not to give up on sharing Jesus but instead to get things right with God. God has provided the process of repentance, forgiveness, and reformation to enable us to clear our relationship with Him and move out once again in speaking of Him.

Jesus said, "If anyone desires to come after Me, let him deny himself, and take up his cross, and follow Me" (Matthew 16:24). To deny ourselves means to turn from the sins that we delight in. To take up His cross and follow Him means to obey Him by sharing God's love in a needy world.

TO TELL THE TRUTH

When I share Jesus with individuals or groups (such as the Hell's Angels and terrorists I mentioned earlier), I could embellish my testimony to make it seem more dramatic. I could describe myself as being older than seven years when I was saved, with a hardened nature and a long history of committing terrible sins. I could say that my salvation shook me mightily, instantly changing my character as from night to day, instead of being the peaceful experience it actually was.

I *could* embellish, but that would be wrong, not to mention counterproductive. We should always tell the simple truth when sharing our testimony with others. The truth is powerful; lying is weak.

I have known people who smoked a little pot before coming to Christ, and as they have told their testimony, their drug use gets worse and worse until you would believe they had been addicted to heroin. Likewise, someone who had a brush with the law, after telling the story again and again, might leave the impression that he was a brutal criminal who did hard time in jail.

~

Don't be ashamed of your testimony, however tame it might seem to you.

~

People who embellish this way might get the reaction of "Wow!" from others that they are looking for. But that doesn't mean they are having anymore impact on them for Christ's cause. And I have observed that, over time, they tend to fall away from Christ themselves because they are living a lie.

Don't be ashamed of your testimony, however tame it might seem to you. Just tell it truthfully and naturally. When you embellish your testimony, you lose its power because it is not real in your heart. So just let your testimony be your testimony—that's all you need.

Even if you do have a dramatic testimony, don't dwell on its worldly aspects. There's no need to go into graphic detail about your former sin; a general statement about it is sufficient. For instance, no one needs to know any details about your former sexual promiscuity. We don't need to know how much money you made selling drugs. We just need to know that you admit to being a sinner who was saved by the mercy of God.

Now, there may be some exceptions. For example, when a former prostitute is sharing Jesus with prostitutes, she most likely will choose to let them know that she used to be where they are. But even in a situation like this, the purpose remains glorifying Christ, not glorifying sin.

A lot of the problems with embellishing testimonies come in when people don't plan ahead of time what they are going to say. They wing it and then they get carried away. That's why I encourage you to write down your testimony in advance. Prayerfully decide what to include in your testimony, every detail true to the facts.

Actually, I recommend that you prepare three versions of your testimony: short, medium, and long.

Let's say you are talking with a stranger on the street, and you think you may have very little time to discuss Jesus with this person. In that case, you may want to share your testimony in just a minute or two. That's your short version.

Your medium-length version may come in handy in a situation such as when you are having lunch with a friend who is an unbeliever. Here you might want to give your testimony in five minutes or so, offering some more background and details.

Finally, you may have a chance to have an extended conversation with an unbeliever. For example, you may be on a plane trip overseas, and you and your seatmate have nothing better to do than to talk for hours. Here you will be free to give the full-length version of your testimony, explaining exactly what happened when you were saved and what your life with Jesus has been like.

After writing down the three versions of your testimony, practice sharing them with a friend. Get his or her feedback, then practice some more until you feel comfortable sharing each version. The next step is simply to get out there and share your testimony with someone who needs Jesus. This is the best "practice" of all!

ATTRACTED OR REPELLED

My wife, Denise, came to Christ when she was crying in a London park, on the brink of despair, and an African lady came up to see if she was okay and then told her how she could know Jesus. In a nutshell, that's her testimony. But she also has an anti-testimony—a story of how believers failed to bring her to Christ.

Years earlier, when Denise was studying in Cambridge, she stepped into the room of a fellow student and saw a Bible by her bed. The other young woman became embarrassed and tried to hide the Bible. But Denise was truly interested in this book, so she kept asking about it. The timid follower of Christ admitted that she studied the Bible but said she didn't want to talk about it.

On another occasion, a work colleague shared about a Bible study that she was hosting at her home and said that the group would be meeting soon. But when Denise asked if she could attend, the woman said, "Oh, it is only for Christians." Denise was crushed and never did join that group of Christians. She went on to conduct her own spiritual search, resorting to the New Age, the occult, and other falsehoods that began a destructive pattern in her life.

The young college student and the work colleague did many things wrong when they had prime opportunities to share Jesus with Denise. For one thing, their attitude was all wrong. When we are sharing Jesus, we should project an image of love for others as well as excitement about their coming to know Jesus.

When you are sharing Jesus, smile. Be positive. Laugh with others. Be friendly and show an interest. Let your face shine with joy. And as you act this way around unbelievers, they will be drawn to you and—more importantly—to Christ. There is power in passion, and we want the glory of God to come through in our lives.

The fact is, people can sense from your disposition what your relationship with God is like. Your attitude will either be attractive, drawing others toward Jesus, or it will be repulsive, pushing them away. And more than that, people will *remember* what impression you leave.

I've known unbelievers who have said such things as "You know, my roommate in college talked to me about Jesus. He was a great guy, too; treated me well." This unbeliever did not get saved back in college, but his experience was a positive one and so he remained open to hearing more about Jesus. That's what can happen when we are loving and gracious toward people.

On the other hand, I have known people who somewhere along the line met followers of Jesus who were grim or prideful or condemning. As a result, they became closed to any mention of Jesus. Getting them to consider His claims further is uphill work.

May we always be people who help others open up more to Jesus.

Now, I realize that no matter how friendly and winsome our attitude is some people will reject Christ. After all, the cross of Christ is a "stumbling block" or "foolishness" to many (1 Corinthians 1:23). But we should always strive to see that, if offense is taken, it is because of the cross and not because of us.

As I have carried a cross around the world, many have come up to me with belligerent attitudes. But that's okay—that's the "offense of the cross" (Galatians 5:11). I try to joke and laugh with them and get them to talk with me about Jesus, for then I might be able to help them see what the cross can really mean to them.

Even when unbelievers choose not to receive Jesus, so long as our presentation is a positive one, it gives them hope. As they see our sincerity, they become convinced that at least *we* believe in Jesus. Maybe, they think, they ought to give Him another chance. They are on the road to trusting in God's Son.

This is the power of a personal testimony when it is truthful and loving. It helps people to see that our lives have been changed by Jesus and that theirs can be too. It opens them up to our sharing with them how they can come to know Jesus for themselves—and then have their own testimony of Jesus.

Begin sharing your personal testimony today!

❧❧❧

QUESTIONS TO CONSIDER

- What points should you cover in the long, medium, and short versions of your testimony?

- When you are giving your testimony, how can you make your manner more appealing?

- What unbeliever will be the first person you give your testimony to?

7

SHARING
JESUS

*I will teach transgressors Your ways, and
sinners shall be converted to You.*

—Psalm 51:13

One day in 1995, while in New Zealand, I was carrying the cross beside a highway that followed the seacoast. Suddenly, up ahead, I heard a scream. It came from a woman who looked to be about thirty-five years old and who was wearing jogging clothes. She had come from the beach and was racing toward me, crying out, "The cross! The cross!"

As she neared me, she asked in a breathless voice, "What are you carrying the cross for?"

I could tell she was upset, and I feared it might be because she did not like the cross of Jesus. But regardless, I began telling her about my journey of carrying the cross around the world.

Before I got far, though, she stopped me and told me her story.

For years, this woman had lived in Wellington, one of the major cities of New Zealand. But in time, people in her life had disappointed her, her dreams had been shattered, and her spirit had become sunk in depression. So two years earlier she had moved to a cottage by the sea in this remote part of the nation, hoping she would find peace. But in those two years, her life had gotten no better. She was in despair.

On this day, she told me, she had planned to run into the sea and drown herself. But before doing so, she had cried out to heaven, "God—if there is a God—I need life! Show me a sign." Just then she looked up and saw my cross!

The woman said to me, "I have come to the cross. I need life." And she burst into tears.

I began to share with her. "We are all sinners and fall short of the glory of God. But God loved us so much that Jesus came to this earth, born of the Virgin Mary, and lived without sin and overcame sin. Jesus did mighty works and showed His power over all the universe.

"Jesus suffered and died on the cross for our sins. He was buried and was raised on the third day. Many saw Jesus alive during the next weeks, and then He ascended into heaven.

"Jesus lives today, and He will hear your prayer if you call out to Him. Jesus will come into your life and will give you a new birth. The Holy Spirit will live within you, and you will have peace with God and be a part of the family of God forever."

I then held the woman's hand and prayed for her. Next, I asked her to repeat after me a prayer: "Dear God, I need You. I believe Jesus died on the cross for my sins and for me. As best I know how, I welcome Jesus into my life and repent of my sins. Jesus, save me and make my home in heaven. I forgive everyone and want to live with You, Jesus, now and forever. Please give me eternal life now. Thank You, Jesus!"

I will never forget her shining, tear-filled eyes and smiling face as she looked at me and said, "Now I have life."

Then I shared with her some scriptures to help her know what Jesus had done in her life, to give her assurance of His continuing presence, and to encourage her to grow in her walk with Jesus and get into a good church.

I look forward to the day when we will meet again in heaven and will celebrate life for eternity.

THE BIG QUESTION

In this chapter, I will relate to you how I normally share Jesus with people. But please don't take what I have to tell you as a formula that you must use. Each situation is a little different; each person is at a little different place spiritually. Be prepared to use the suggestions I give you, but remain open to the Holy Spirit's leading in each opportunity you have.

Sometimes (though by no means always) I begin with what I call the Big Question: "Should you die right now, do you have the assurance that you would go to heaven?" I call this the Big Question because it really does deal with the biggest issue in our lives: where will we spend eternity? I have discovered through long experience that the Big Question gets people in all kinds of life situations to think seriously about their lives. It focuses on eternity and brings us face to face with Jesus.

There are basically three possible answers to the Big Question: *yes, no,* or *I don't know.* Should someone answer the question with *no* or *I don't know,* I say, "I want to show you from the Word of God how you can know that you will go to heaven when you die." I have found that almost everyone will let me go ahead and share about Jesus at that point.

Should someone answer *yes,* then I generally say, "Wonderful! Upon what do you base that? How do you know that you will go to heaven?"

~

Should I get a response like "I'm basically a good person," I never criticize the other person or try to correct him or her.

~

In a case like this, the other person might explain that he or she has trusted in Christ alone for salvation. And that's great—then we're dealing with a precious brother or sister in Christ. On the other hand, we might get an answer like "Well, I'm basically a good person" or "I go to church." The other thinks that his or her morality or religion is good enough to earn God's acceptance. This person is working under a false premise.

Should I get a response like "I'm basically a good person," I never criticize the other person or try to correct him or her. I never say, "No, that's not how it works!" Instead, I say, "I want to show you from the Word of God how you can know that you will go to heaven when you die."

THE JESUS STORY

Many people in this world do not know even the basic facts about the life of Jesus. And they cannot trust in Jesus when they don't know who He is. So the more we talk about Jesus, the more convicting our sharing will be.

When I sense that the person I am speaking with knows little or nothing about Jesus, I like to give him or her a brief summary of Jesus' life—how and why He was born, how He taught people and performed miracles, how He died, was resurrected, and ascended to heaven. In fact, I give a complete overview of the life of Jesus.

One time, in Scotland, I was sharing with a university student who felt a need for new life. So I explained to her about the life and death of Christ, and then proceeded to invite her to pray with me, asking Jesus to come into her heart.

She asked, "How can a dead man help me?"

That's when I realized that I had neglected to tell her about Jesus' resurrection! I corrected the omission, and then she was ready to pray with me. But I learned something that day: always cover *all* the key points about Jesus.

Sharing about Jesus' life, death, and resurrection is just what His early followers did. They did not have the New Testament (it hadn't been written yet), so they merely went around and told people what they knew about Jesus. And think about how many people became followers of Jesus through their efforts!

There is nothing more powerful than the story of Jesus. Review it for yourself by reading the Gospels: Matthew, Mark, Luke, and John. Then think about how you can clearly and effectively relate it to others.

I suggest you have a shorter version and a longer version of the story of Jesus that you can use. Sometimes you may have only a limited time with a person, and at other times you can talk about Jesus for a long time. Let the Holy Spirit lead you in this. The important thing is to make sure that the other person knows the life and message of Jesus so that he or she can then know Jesus personally.

STEPS TO GOD

You're not a theologian and I'm not a theologian, but we both can understand and teach the basic message of salvation in Jesus Christ our Lord. It's so simple and yet so profound. Using plain, everyday words, we can convey to an interested person how God has reached out to us in love through His Son to save us from the consequences of our sin.

1. We are sinners. "All have sinned, and come short of the glory of God" (Romans 3:23, KJV).

We all have a problem, and it's called sin. But rather than being condemning of others, when sharing with another person, I start with me. In a calm voice I say, "I am a sinner and you are a sinner. All people are sinners."

I point to the biblical definition of sin—it's right there in Romans 3:23. We come short of the glory of God. Certainly, we may be good people in a lot of ways, but we don't come anywhere near to living up to the glory of Almighty God.

What is the glory of God? Well, in human terms, the glory of God is reflected perfectly only in Jesus. *He* is the glory of God. So when we say we are sinners, we are saying that we don't measure up to the standard of Jesus. Most people whom I have talked with have no problem admitting their sinfulness when it is described like that.

The point of all this is to recognize that there is a consequence to sin.

2. Our sin separates us from God. "The wages of sin is death" (Romans 6:23).

Just as a roof separates us from the sky when we're inside a building, so our sin separates us from God. Because God is all holy, He cannot tolerate sin. He cannot accept sinners unless their sins have been washed away. To be separated from the source of true spiritual life—God—is to be spiritually dead.

To quote it in full, Romans 6:23 says, "The wages of sin is death, but the gift of God is eternal life in Christ

Jesus our Lord." Many times, when I'm talking with a person, I'll draw two lines side by side. I'll put "Satan, sin, wages, death" on one side and "God, gift, eternal life through Jesus" on the other side, with a space between the two sets of terms. Unforgiven sinners are on the side of Satan and sin, separated by a gulf from God.

What is the difference between wages and a gift? Well, imagine that you worked hard for a week and then on Friday your boss said, "Here is some money—it's my gift to you." Wouldn't you respond with something like "Hey, that's no gift; I earned it"? You would be right to do so. A wage is something we earn, while a gift is something we receive.

We deserve spiritual death because of our sin, but eternal life is something we can only receive through Jesus. We can't earn eternal life through doing good works or by being religious or in any other way. But Jesus Christ has earned it for us and freely offers it to us.

3. Christ died for us. "While we were still sinners, Christ died for us" (Romans 5:8).

As you tell an unbeliever the story of Jesus, you should emphasize the importance of Jesus' death. It was central to the meaning of His life, and it is central to ours, for at the cross Jesus took upon Himself the penalty for our sin. This is how eternal life has become a gift available through Jesus Christ.

Going back to my diagram, I often like to add a cross bridging the gap between spiritual death and spiritual life. The cross of Christ is how we cross over from spiritual death to spiritual life. In fact, it is the *only* way to get from one side to the other.

Each of us must individually choose to make that journey. It is a journey we make by the faith that God gives us or not at all.

4. Through trusting in Jesus, we can be saved. "Whoever calls on the name of the LORD shall be saved" (Romans 10:13).

We each must decide whether we will make Christ's sacrifice on the cross apply to us, personally, by putting our trust in Him. We agree that we are sinners and that Jesus is the one and only Son of God, who died and rose for us. We believe in Him and commit our lives to Him forever. We repent and call on Him, and He saves us.

~

The point is that we show from the Word of God what trust in Jesus can do for us....

~

I try not to get hung up on the terminology. Sometimes I use "be saved"; other times, "be born again" or "accept Jesus" or "receive Jesus" or "become a follower of Jesus." These are all good, biblical terms. I use whichever wording seems to communicate best with a person. The point is that we show from the Word of God what trust in Jesus can do for us—rescue us from our sins, cause us to be born of the Spirit, and give us a place in God's kingdom.

Sometimes when you're sharing Jesus and the new life in Him, the other person might go off on a tangent. In a case like that, gently bring the discussion back to Jesus and the cross. You don't need to discuss evolution or morality or politics. Paul, a witness of Jesus in the early church, said it this way: "I determined not to know any-thing among you except Jesus Christ and Him crucified" (1 Corinthians 2:2).

When someone asks you a question you don't know the answer for, simply say, "I don't know a lot about that, but I know that Jesus loves us and wants to save us from our sins." Bring it back to Jesus. It's all about Jesus.

THE SINNER'S PRAYER

After you have explained how to believe in and become a follower of Jesus, the person you are speak-ing with will probably be wondering just what he or she has to do to receive eternal life. Explain that all it takes is a simple prayer of repentance. Now, many people have never prayed in any way, or at least have never prayed for forgiveness. So you'll need to encourage them and lead them through the prayer.

Don't make the mistake of trying to judge whether a person is ready to accept Christ yet. You can't know that. Only God and the individual know that. When you have explained to someone how to receive Jesus, just encour-age him or her to take this step of believing in Christ, then start the prayer.

If I'm talking to a woman named Abby (let's say), I might say something like this: "Jesus can come into your life, Abby. You can know Him. Pray this prayer with me. Believe it in your heart and speak it with your mouth. Just say, 'Dear God. ...' "

There is nothing magical about the exact wording of the prayer you use. The main thing is that the other person asks for forgiveness and asks Jesus to come into his or her heart. As a model, here is a prayer I have used for years:

> Dear God, as best I know how, I give You my life. Lord Jesus Christ, forgive all my sins. I believe in You. I repent of my sins and want to follow You. I ask You to come into my heart and be the Lord of my life. I have been wrong; You are right. Take control of my life as I give myself to You. Thank You for hearing my prayer. I forgive everyone. Make my home in heaven and put my name in Your book of life. I love You, Lord. Thank You for hearing my prayer. In Jesus' name I pray, amen.

I like to pray the prayer a phrase at a time and let the other person repeat each phrase after me.

Should the other person not pray the prayer out loud with you, go ahead and pray it anyway. The person may be praying it silently within his or her mind. Or the person may decide to pray it later. In that case, he or she will be learning by listening to you go through the prayer. No matter what, it does no harm to pray the prayer.

Assuming the other person has prayed the prayer with you, then immediately afterward give him or her assurance about what has happened. "God bless you, Abby. God heard your prayer and has forgiven your sins. Jesus has come into your life to stay." Give encouragement. The most important time in a new convert's life is the moment he or she receives Jesus.

In the next chapter we will be looking at how you can help a new believer to walk faithfully with the Lord for a lifetime. But even before you start talking about following Jesus, you can encourage the new believer to share about his or her new life in Jesus with someone else. Should another person be watching what is going on, you might say to the new believer something like this: "Share with your husband (or your friend) here what Jesus just did in your heart."

In cases where the other person is reluctant to start that kind of sharing, you can lead him or her through it. Ask the new believer, "What did you just ask Jesus to do?"

The new believer will probably say, "Well, I asked Him to forgive me."

"He didn't lie when He promised to forgive sins, did He?"

"No."

"So what did He do?"

"He forgave my sins."

"You asked Jesus into your life. What did He do?

"Jesus came into my life!"

The best follow-up for new followers of Jesus is immediate. Having them share their decision reinforces the experience for them and might even lead to another person's coming to Jesus.

~

Remember, there is never failure in sharing Jesus.

~

I urge you to practice going through the scriptures listed above simply and clearly and leading another through the sinner's prayer. Perhaps you have a friend with whom you can take turns practicing these skills before doing it for real with the people you meet in daily life. Keep lifting up Jesus, and He will do the drawing of people into His kingdom.

Remember, there is never failure in sharing Jesus. It's not your kingdom; it's His. Go ahead and share.

KEEPING THE DOOR OPEN

I have been assuming up to this point that the person you are talking with is going along with you and agrees to pray the prayer of salvation. But of course, that is not always the case. You might invite someone to receive Jesus, and he or she will say, "No, thank you. I'm not interested." What do you do then? You respect the other's wishes, but you don't give up.

Let's say you have been sharing with a clerk at the convenience store where you buy your gasoline. Should she turn down your request to pray with you, then say something like "Thank you so much for listening to me. God bless you. I'll be praying that God will meet your every need."

The next time you come to the convenience store, say "God bless you" to the clerk again, and the next time, and the next. Eventually the clerk is likely to say something like "You know, it's really nice to hear you say those words. I look forward to you coming in."

That's your opening to try again. You can now say, "Well, God really does love you. That's why Christ died for you." You have the opportunity to explain the message of Jesus to her one more time. And this time the clerk may be more receptive.

Handle the follow-up however you judge best, as you listen to the Holy Spirit, but my point is this: don't slam the door on the person. Keep it open all the time. Pray, be a friend, and look for another opportunity that the Holy Spirit will give you.

Ron Bozarth ran five topless nightclubs and finally the famous Comedy Store in Hollywood, California. I shared Jesus with him and we were friends for nine years. He let me preach on stage in his nightclubs, but he would always put off making a full commitment to Jesus.

But then, in 1976, he asked me to perform the wedding for him and his bride, Geri. At the ceremony, I invited the couple to receive Jesus—and they did! In front of all their Hollywood entertainment friends, they got down on their knees and fully gave their lives to Jesus to love and follow Him.

It took nine years with Ron, but I didn't give up. Neither should you give up sharing with your friends and acquaintances. Don't slam the door. Don't cut somebody off. Keep offering the invitation of Christ.

Sometimes we sow seed and sometimes we harvest. Certainly we should expect to harvest every time we talk to people about Jesus, but we don't know for sure. The important thing for us to remember is that we have never failed when we have faithfully presented Jesus and His message of love and eternal life. Whether the other person responds immediately or not, so long as we have done our part we've acted to glorify God. Depend on the Holy Spirit to convict the other person, and keep your heart full of love. Remember, it's all about Jesus, His life, His Kingdom, and His love.

∽∽∽

QUESTIONS TO CONSIDER

- What ways have you found to be most effective in turning a conversation to the topic of following Jesus?

- If someone asked you, "What are the most important things to know about Jesus?" what would you say?

- How would you word a prayer for salvation so that it seems the most natural and straightforward to you?

- What kind of practice or preparation would make you more ready to share Jesus with one who needs Him?

8

MAKING LIFELONG FOLLOWERS OF JESUS

[Paul] went over the region of Galatia and Phrygia in order, strengthening all the disciples.

—Acts 18:23

Jesus commanded, "Go therefore and make *disciples* of all the nations" (Matthew 28:19, emphasis added). He didn't say, "Make *converts* of all the nations." We don't want people merely to pray a prayer inviting Jesus into their hearts; we want them to become lifelong followers of Jesus. That's what it means to be a disciple. Therefore, sharing Jesus with people includes not only sharing how to be saved in Jesus but also sharing how to live for Jesus.

Follow-up with a new believer is something that any follower of Jesus can do. At least we can get the process started for the persons we have led to Christ. Even though we may not be experts in doctrine, we can introduce them to Scripture and share the basics of living for Jesus so that new believers can begin to be more grounded, spiritually. We can set them on their way to a wonderful life in the Savior.

It is important for someone, after being born into the family of God, to grow in knowledge and understanding of how to truly follow Jesus. This is what I call follow-up. As the new convert matures, he or she becomes strong and will bear a plentiful harvest of fruit for the glory of God.

Helping those who have put their trust in Jesus to begin a life spent in His love is a privilege and a joy. These people are our new brothers and sisters. We are welcoming them into the family! Our desire should be to follow up with them faithfully and effectively.

Before I can go any further on this subject, however, I need to deal with an objection that seems inevitably to come up.

TRUSTING GOD FOR THE FOLLOW-UP

I've heard it over and over again from dear fellow believers in Christ. "If we aren't going to be able to do extended discipleship with people who pray to receive Jesus, then we shouldn't even share Jesus with them. They'll just fall away."

On the surface, this attitude might sound realistic, even wise. But do you see what it does? It shrinks the sphere within which we are willing to share Jesus until it includes little more than our family and closest friends. The person sitting next to us on a bus, the neighbor we eat with at a barbecue, the acquaintance we meet at a business conference—all such people are no longer candidates for us to speak with about the Savior.

I take no pleasure in saying this, but I must. Those who let the inability to do extensive teaching of new believers prevent them from talking with others about the good news of salvation in Jesus are at best misguided. At worst they are using their argument as an excuse to make a guilt-free escape from sharing Jesus with people who need Him.

But don't take my word for it. Consider how Jesus Himself shared the truths about salvation. Was He restrictive in whom He chose to discuss God with? Supposing he had been, He would never have left His hometown and His neighbors there. But in reality, He traveled the highways of Israel and its neighboring lands, touching large numbers of people day after day.

If Jesus had been following the modern teaching on follow-up of new believers, He would have said yes to the former demoniac of Gerasa when that man begged to travel with Him. But what really happened? "Jesus did not permit him, but said to him, 'Go home to your friends, and tell them what great things the Lord has done for you'" (Mark 5:19).

And what happened when Philip brought the Ethiopian eunuch to a point of trusting in Jesus and being baptized? "When they came up out of the water, the Spirit of the Lord caught Philip away, so that the eunuch saw him no more" (Acts 8:39).

We don't know what happened to the Gerasene, the Ethiopian, and many others who committed their lives to Jesus after a brief initial contact with someone. But we can trust that God had another way of leading them closer to Him. The first person to touch their lives for God did not need to be the same person who gave them extensive follow-up teaching.

Can we not trust God to build up the people we introduce to His Son? After all, He loves them more than we do. Since He is capable of saving people from their sins, He is certainly able to see that they learn how to live a life that pleases Him, even when we are not able to do it.

That's the way it is within the church of Christ. It is a worldwide body made up of diverse members whom God coordinates to accomplish His work in the world. Therefore, it is presumptuous of us to assume that only we ourselves are going to be able to instruct someone we lead to Christ.

After the tent meeting when I was seven, I never again saw the evangelist who helped me pray to receive Christ. Nevertheless, I managed to learn what it means to follow Jesus. My parents, my childhood church, and countless others over the years have taught and encouraged me.

And I have seen the same dynamic at work over and over again as I have traveled the world. Many times I have shared Jesus only briefly with people, perhaps when I met them on the road or when spending the night in their home. Yet fairly regularly I get e-mails or phone calls from these people, telling me that they are still following Jesus.

In the previous chapter I told how I witnessed for Christ with the nightclub owner Ron Bozarth for nine years before he fully came to Christ with his wife, Geri, at their wedding. Well, here's the rest of the story.

After the wedding ceremony, I encouraged Ron and Geri in following Jesus, then left to go on a cross-walking trip. I was gone for a year overseas. When I returned, I went to one of the nightclubs where Ron had been the manager when he came to Jesus. I asked for the manager, and someone other than Ron came to me. When I asked him where Ron was, the new manager said, "Oh, haven't you heard? Ron's got religion and he doesn't work here anymore."

~

God will follow up, never fear.

~

It took me several days of searching before I found Ron and Geri. They had left Hollywood and had spent the last year studying the Bible. They then started a Bible study in their home, and that in turn became Christ Fellowship Community Church in Lake Forest, California, where they have now pastored for more than twenty-five years. We remain close and dear friends.

God will follow up, never fear.

By no means am I opposed to people getting a thorough grounding in the things of God. Let me repeat that I think follow-up is the necessary second half of sharing Jesus. My point is simply that we should never put so much emphasis on follow-up that we let it hinder us from sharing with people in the first place about the good news of salvation in Jesus.

THE NEW LIFE OF A JESUS FOLLOWER

Just as there is no single way to share about salvation that is best in every situation, so there is no single way of doing follow-up that is always best. Rely on the Spirit's leading to show you how God would want you to help establish a new believer in a life with Jesus. Meanwhile, let me share a few general truths and tips that I have discovered over the years.

The best follow-up is done immediately after people trust in Jesus. This is when they are both most receptive and most needy. After all, stumbling blocks and temptations often come in the early days of a person's life with Jesus. Whatever we can do to prepare a new believer to go through these trials will help to establish him or her as a faithful, lifelong follower of Jesus.

Right after congratulating new believers on the start of their life in Jesus, we should begin sharing a few basics about their walk with Jesus. We can't assume that they will know what to do next. They may know next to nothing about the Bible, about the church, or about many other things we older followers of Jesus take for granted. How much you choose to say will depend on the situation.

In my travels around the world, I have often shared Jesus with people whom I was able to speak with for just an evening or an hour or even less. After they have received Jesus, I have shared with them a few key points they needed to know to begin a life with Jesus. You, too, may sometimes be dealing with people you will never see again. Then again, sometimes we have an ongoing relationship with a new believer. Whatever the length of time we have to spend with someone, our purpose is to follow up with them to the extent we can.

In fact, I believe that when a church has a team to share Jesus for salvation in their community, they ought also to have a team to do follow-up. (It may be the same people; it may not.) This second team can go back to people who have made commitments to Jesus, visit them in their homes, and encourage these new believers. To put it in more traditional words, when we have outreach evangelism, we need outreach discipleship as well.

But regardless of whether you have a team helping you, do what you can to follow up with someone you have introduced to Christ. Whenever possible, don't let the relationship you have established with this person drop. Perhaps you could invite the new believer to have lunch with you or to come over to your home so that you can talk further about the life of a Jesus follower.

When you're talking to a stranger, ask for a phone number, a home address, or an e-mail address so that you can follow up later. You should be cautious in doing this, however, when the new believer is someone of the opposite sex. A man who has led a woman to Jesus, for example, might choose to invite the new believer to call a female friend of his who is a follower of Jesus.

When you're talking with people who live in your hometown, invite them to your church or your small-group Bible study with you. And by this, I don't mean that you should just give them the address of the church and the service time. Offer to pick them up or at least to meet them at the church door. When you say, "Come and sit with me," they will feel that they have a friend and they will be much less intimidated by the idea of going to church.

One of the best things you can do for a new believer is to give him or her a Bible. With the Word of God in hand, this person can now grow. The Word of God will help to direct this person's paths in the ways of our Lord Jesus.

⁓

Should you be a relatively new believer yourself and not know much about the Bible, don't let that stop you.

⁓

You could also offer to begin a one-on-one Bible study with a new believer, perhaps reading through one of the Gospels together. Should you be a relatively new believer yourself and not know much about the Bible, don't let that stop you. After all, you are offering to study the Bible *with* the other person. You can both learn together!

The point is to maintain fellowship with a new believer and be responsible for him or her to whatever extent you can.

The other day I felt moved by God's Spirit to call a man I led to Jesus a few months earlier. It turns out that in the meantime he had run into some followers of Jesus who did not represent Jesus very well. It had discouraged him. So I was able to encourage him to stay focused on Christ, not on Christ's hypocritical followers.

I saw this man in church just the other day—he's still following Jesus. But who knows what would have happened to this new believer if I had not kept in touch? This is what follow-up does. It is the means by which fellow servants of Jesus keep each other on the path that God would have us walk.

Whatever our preferred strategy and whatever length of time we have to share with a new believer, there are a few key points we should try to cover, if at all possible. These have to do with what a new believer should *know* and what he should *do*.

WHAT A NEW BELIEVER SHOULD KNOW

When a person has received Christ, what does that really mean? A new believer may not know. And that's why we need to explain it.

This is not about gaining head knowledge. Rather, it is about establishing a person's life in Jesus. You see, while the day a person receives Christ is a wonderful time, it is also a vulnerable time. When people first put their trust in Jesus, our spiritual enemy moves in to try to discourage them and make them doubt their salvation. And they have few defenses against him.

Imagine that you have led a man named Michael to Christ. Afterward, Michael drives home, gets stuck in traffic, and starts cursing. What is he going to think? Quite possibly, Michael will begin to wonder whether anything has really changed inside him. After all, he is acting just the way he did before.

We need to help new believers understand that, just because they are followers of Jesus, that doesn't mean they are perfect. Jesus in them is perfect, and God is working at perfecting them, but they will fail. At first they are taking baby steps. As they get stronger, spiritually speaking, they will be able to walk and even run. Certainly they should try not to sin, but when they do, they should fall into the arms of Jesus, not fall out of them.

For reasons like this, we need to help new believers understand what has happened to them. Here are key points we should help a new believer grasp right away:

1. *Jesus has come to live within your heart.* Jesus said, "Behold, I stand at the door and knock. If anyone hears My voice and opens the door, I will come in to him and dine with him, and he with Me" (Revelation 3:20).

When we open the door (our will) to Jesus, He comes into our heart to stay. In other words, we have a personal relationship with God through His Son. We can come to Him with our every need and receive His victory. The One who has made us now comes to live within us.

2. *Your sins are forgiven.* "If we confess our sins, [Jesus] is faithful and just to forgive us our sins and to cleanse us from all unrighteousness" (1 John 1:9).

The Bible teaches that, when we repent, the blood of Jesus Christ cleanses us from all our sin. Repenting is turning our backs on the old way, putting our trust in Jesus, and desiring to live for Him from now on. When we repent and ask forgiveness, our sins are gone. Other people may remember our failings, but God erases the errors of our past.

3. You are saved. "If you confess with your mouth the Lord Jesus and believe in your heart that God has raised Him from the dead, you will be saved. For with the heart one believes unto righteousness, and with the mouth confession is made unto salvation. For 'whoever calls on the name of the LORD shall be saved' " (Romans 10:9-10, 13).

To be saved means to be delivered from spiritual death through putting trust in Jesus Christ. Sin separates us from God, but Jesus bore our sins on the cross and paid the eternal penalty for our sins. When we receive Jesus, we are saved from the penalty of sin, which is eternal separation from God. We are being saved daily from the power of Satan, and one day in heaven we will be completely saved from the presence of Satan and of sin.

4. You have received eternal life. "God so loved the world that He gave His only begotten Son, that whoever believes in Him should not perish but have everlasting life" (John 3:16).

Before we received Christ, we were spiritually dead. But now, in Christ, we are spiritually alive. This is not a temporary kind of life but an eternal life in Jesus. He is with us every moment, beginning with the time when we received Him into our hearts. He has promised never to leave us or forsake us.

5. *You are a child of God.* "As many as received [Jesus], to them He gave the right to become children of God" (John 1:12).

Through faith in Jesus Christ, we are now in the family of God. We are the objects of God's love and can be sure that our relationship with Him is close, personal, and intimate. As a good father loves his children and cares for them, so God our heavenly Father now loves and cares for us.

6. *The Holy Spirit abides within you.* "Do you not know that your body is the temple of the Holy Spirit who is in you, whom you have from God, and you are not your own? For you were bought at a price; therefore glorify God in your body and in your spirit, which are God's" (1 Corinthians 6:19-20).

God has revealed Himself to us as the Father, the Son, and the Holy Spirit. He comes to live within us at the moment when we trust in Jesus, making our body His dwelling place. Through the Holy Spirit, the fruits of the Spirit-filled life—love, joy, peace, longsuffering, kindness, goodness, faithfulness, gentleness, self-control—can become a living reality (Galatians 5:22-23).

7. *You have become a new person.* "If anyone is in Christ, he is a new creation; old things have passed away;

behold, all things have become new" (2 Corinthians 5:17).

Sometimes people call the time when they trusted in Jesus their "new birth day"—and with good reason. Inwardly, each believer has become a new person. Jesus Christ changes the heart. The outward actions of our lives then are changed as God's Spirit lives within us.

WHAT A NEW BELIEVER SHOULD DO

There is nothing we can do to earn God's love; that love comes as a gift. Religious practices can even interfere with our relationship with God, if we undertake them with the wrong motives. Still, the Bible teaches several actions or habits that are capable of drawing us nearer to Jesus.

The biblical practices are ones that all of us, regardless of how long we have been following Jesus, ought to be reflecting in our lives. So we should make sure that we ourselves are being obedient, even as we encourage new believers to begin incorporating the following behaviors into their life with Jesus.

1. Pray daily. "Pray without ceasing" (1 Thessalonians 5:17).

Prayer is a moment-by-moment relationship with God. We can pray at any time, at any place. As we share every need of our lives with God in prayer, we can know that He hears us. Prayer is also being open for God to speak to us. It is in this most personal way, through prayer, that we grow spiritually day by day.

2. *Read the Bible daily.* "[The blessed man's] delight is in the law of the LORD, and in His law he meditates day and night" (Psalm 1:2).

Jesus said, "Man shall not live by bread alone, but by every word that proceeds from the mouth of God" (Matthew 4:4). We need to eat the spiritual food of God's Word (the Bible) daily, to study His Word, and to obey His commandments.

3. *Share Jesus daily.* "You shall receive power when the Holy Spirit has come upon you; and you shall be witnesses to Me ... to the end of the earth" (Acts 1:8).

We are saved to share our faith, not simply to wait until Jesus comes to receive us into His kingdom. Our commission is to go into all the world and preach the good news about Jesus to every person. We should seek to share Him with every person we meet wherever we are. We should not be fearful or timid, but we should be loving and open as we speak with others of Jesus.

4. *Confess Christ openly and be baptized.* "Those who gladly received his word were baptized" (Acts 2:41).

Jesus has asked us to confess Him openly and follow Him in baptism after we have put our faith in Him as Savior. Baptism does not wash away our sin, but it is a public testimony that we have died to our old way of life so that we may live a new life with Jesus.

5. Attend church where the Bible is preached and Christ is honored. "Let us consider one another in order to stir up love and good works, not forsaking the assembling of ourselves together, as is the manner of some, but exhorting one another" (Hebrews 10:24-25).

Every follower of Jesus should be in fellowship with other believers, praying, singing, worshiping, studying the Bible, following Christ's commandments, and seeking to share Jesus and minister to the needs of others. It is vital that we assemble with others to grow spiritually ourselves and to help others. This fellowship can be found in many churches and also in small Bible study and prayer groups.

6. Keep Christ's commandments. "If you love Me, keep My commandments" (John 14:15).

We obey the commandments of Jesus, and the rest of God's commandments in the Bible, because we *want* to. A person who loves Jesus desires to be obedient to His will and accepts that the way the Bible has asked us to live is right and proper for us. Therefore, we seek daily to live as He has asked us to live.

7. Love others. "This is [God's] commandment: that we should believe on the name of His Son Jesus Christ and love one another" (1 John 3:23).

As God has loved us, so we should love others. We should forgive others when they treat us badly. We should share the material things that God has blessed us with. We should be concerned about the whole of a person—body, mind, and soul—and seek in every way to meet the needs of others.

8. *Be filled with the Holy Spirit.* "Do not be drunk with wine, in which is dissipation; but be filled with the Spirit" (Ephesians 5:18).

~

To be filled with the Holy Spirit is to have a moment-by-moment walk with God.

~

When we are saved, the Holy Spirit comes to live within us, yet often we are not fully under the control of God's Spirit. To be filled with the Holy Spirit is to have a moment-by-moment walk with God. When we realize that any attitude or action of ours is not of God, then at that moment we should repent, ask for God's cleansing, and invite Him to refill us with the fullness of His Spirit.

The filling of the Spirit continues the marvelous spiritual adventure begun when we first trusted in Jesus.

THE KEY TO FOLLOW-UP

Although I have described what a new believer ought to know and to do, I must emphasize that these are not ends in themselves. They are means to a greater goal. Discipleship is really all about helping people stay in love with Jesus.

Brand-new followers of Jesus are often radiant with love for Him. Many "mature" Christians, on the other hand, are filled with knowledge of godly things but have lost their first love. In that respect, the new believers are more like Jesus than the older ones. So if discipleship means making new believers take Jesus for granted like the older ones do, then it would be better for the new followers of Jesus not to "mature" at all!

We should encourage new believers in their zeal for Jesus, never quench that zeal. For instance, imagine a new believer who excitedly says, "I want to go tell my brother what just happened to me when I accepted Christ!"

It would be a terrible mistake to say to him, "That's all well and good, but first don't you think you ought to learn something about what the Bible teaches and what we do here at this church?"

You can just hear the new believer responding, "Well ... okay, I guess so," as the energy flows out of him.

No! Let him go and talk to his brother. So what if he doesn't understand much yet? There will be time for teaching him. We should never let that need for teaching, as important as it is, take the glow off a believer's love for his or her newfound Savior.

I say this not just for the sake of the new believers; the rest of us need them and their zeal. Indeed, any church that doesn't have an infusion of new believers quickly becomes static and cold. On the other hand, a church that has a steady inflow of people who have recently found Christ is a church that's filled with life, excitement, freshness. Let us welcome new brothers and sisters and channel their enthusiasm without squelching it.

Follow-up is making the most of a new believer's love for Jesus. Again, it's all about Jesus.

ल ल ल

QUESTIONS TO CONSIDER

- What have you learned about having a growing relationship with Jesus from your own experience?

- What are some areas where you can improve your follow-up with new believers?

- How can you enlist the aid of other Jesus followers to help with follow-up?

PART 3

TIPS TO MAKE YOU MORE
EFFECTIVE

9

EFFECTIVE COMMUNICATION

Unless you utter by the tongue words easy to understand, how will it be known what is spoken? For you will be speaking into the air.
—1 Corinthians 14:9

For a time when I was in college I became legalistic, focusing more on how people were behaving than on whether they had made the choice to follow Jesus. When I was sharing Jesus with someone who was smoking a cigarette, for example, I would challenge him, "Are you prepared to give up smoking?" I hesitated to help people pray to receive Christ unless they had first agreed to turn their back on drinking, dancing, going to the movies, or whatever else in their lifestyle I was down on. It was almost as if I was trying to get a person perfected *before* he or she came to Jesus.

Thankfully, before all this had gone on long, I studied the life of Christ in the Bible and realized that I had gotten my priorities out of balance. Living a clean life is important—there's no question about that. But it is not my job to condemn other people, especially unbelievers, for their actions. My job is simply to introduce others to Jesus and invite them to know Him. Once He comes into their lives, the Holy Spirit will go to work, leading them to change whatever He does not like about their lifestyle.

I was not as effective during my legalistic period as I might otherwise have been, but by the goodness of God, some of the people I spoke with did come to Jesus. That's why I try not to be critical of people who are sharing Jesus in ways I don't think are the best. God is the One who changes lives, after all, and so long as His witnesses are acting faithfully, He will still work through them. Nevertheless, as I look back on my problem with legalism, it reminds me that all of us can learn better ways of sharing Jesus with others.

You may not have a problem with legalism, but I suspect there is another area in which you could improve your communication with unbelievers. Maybe you are too timid, passing up opportunities to share Jesus because the timing doesn't seem right. Maybe you have a tendency to let needy people entangle you in their problems to the point that it hinders your outreach for Jesus. Maybe you put on a formal tone of voice or use highfalutin language that is not natural for you. Whatever the weakness in your approach may be, you can overcome it with God's help.

I have been sharing Jesus for nearly six decades now, and I am still learning how to do it better. May all of us become lifelong learners when it comes to sharing Jesus. After all, we love Him and we want to serve Him in the very best way we can!

COMMUNICATION TIPS

God has gifted each of us differently to share His Son with others. And thank God for those differences! Nevertheless, I have found the following points to be generally true for all who share Jesus with others.

- *Never doubt the spiritual need of an unbeliever.* "There is no difference; for all have sinned and fall short of the glory of God" (Romans 3:22-23).

Some you speak with may not seem to have any spiritual longings. Some may belong to another religion. Some may say they are not interested in Jesus. In one sense, none of that matters. We should never think of an unbeliever, *Well, maybe he (or she) doesn't need Jesus.*

Everybody needs Jesus! All who are outside Christ have a need for His salvation, no matter what they might say to the contrary. They may not realize it yet, or they may want to deny it, but they do have that need.

So speak to a person's spiritual need without any hesitation. Of course, you don't need to dwell on someone's spiritual lostness. It may be enough to say, "I'm a sinner and you're a sinner," and then move on. But you ought never to harbor doubt about a person's need for Jesus.

Similarly, we should not judge whether we ought to continue talking about Jesus based upon the other person's apparent emotional reaction. After all, some people can be highly demonstrative, weeping and crying out, while others show no emotion at all. It doesn't matter. We don't need to judge by body language how someone is reacting. As long as the other person is still listening, we should go on with our conversation about Jesus and encourage the other to trust in Him.

- *Don't wait for the ideal situation.* "Preach the word! Be ready in season and out of season" (2 Timothy 4:2).

Sometimes, when I learn that a fellow believer is not sharing Jesus with others, I will ask why that is.

"Well, the Lord isn't leading me," this person might say.

"How do you know He's not?"

"Because I haven't felt Him telling me to talk to somebody."

Felt? What are they waiting for—for a tingling up their spine or for their left foot to start twitching?

We don't need to feel any specific leading in order to share Jesus with others. In fact, we should assume that God wants us to talk to others about His Son every opportunity we get unless He tells us not to. When we think we must wait for an ideal situation—a time when it's convenient for us, the other person seems interested, and we have plenty of time to talk—we'll do very little sharing, because the ideal situation hardly ever comes around.

Maybe your waitress is having a busy day. That's okay—share with her quickly. Maybe someone seems resistant. Don't let that stop you—inside maybe he's aching for hope in his life. Take every opportunity you get to share Jesus, however fleeting or unpromising it might seem.

As we take on the attitude that we don't need an ideal situation, we will share Jesus in every situation to the best of our ability as God gives us grace. He blesses our willing and persistent intention to represent Him.

- *Think through what you might say.* "Let your speech always be with grace, seasoned with salt, that you may know how you ought to answer each one" (Colossians 4:6).

~

The Holy Spirit can lead us in our preparation and in how we make use of that preparation.

~

We have talked about the importance of being led by the Spirit as we share Jesus. But there is no reason why that should keep us from preparing what we say. The Holy Spirit can lead us in our preparation and in how we make use of that preparation. Indeed, just as the apostle Paul asked his fellow believers to pray that God would give him the right words to speak (Ephesians 6:19-20), so we can pray that God will teach us what we ought to say.

Then we can go through in our minds what we will say. For example, while we are lying in bed at night, or when we wake up early one morning, we can think through what we might say and how we might say it. We will feel more ready and more confident in a witnessing situation when we have prepared what we will say.

- *Recognize your personal style of sharing Jesus.* "The body is not one member but many" (1 Corinthians 12:14).

I'm not asking you to adopt my style—or anyone else's for that matter. The best style for you is your own.

Some people are highly assertive; others take a quieter approach. Some people like to start with the Big Question ("Should you die right now, do you have the assurance that you would go to heaven?"); others start by asking whether they can pray for another person. Some people like to follow a script; others prefer to wing it. The possible variations are almost endless. How do *you* like to share Jesus?

One advantage of sharing Jesus frequently is that it helps you learn what you are comfortable with. Reflect on your sharing experiences and get feedback from a fellow believer about what has seemed to work best for you. God will lead you in finding the approach or approaches that are most effective in your case.

- *Communicate in a way that people will understand.* "Unless you utter by the tongue words easy to understand, how will it be known what is spoken?" (1 Corinthians 14:9).

Many people who know my history associate me with the hippie era in California. I'm known for having told people to "turn on to Jesus" and for calling God "psychedelic," for example. What some people don't know, however, is that I came from the Deep South and had to *learn* the hippie jargon in order to use it in reaching young people in California. Then, when I started traveling around the world, I had to unlearn that jargon because it didn't work in other places. In fact, I have continued to learn how to speak effectively with different people about Jesus.

I don't blame unbelievers when they don't respond positively to my message about Jesus. Instead, I use their response as an opportunity to ask myself how I could share Jesus better. After all, it's not that people don't have a need for Jesus. Many spend their whole evening at a bar pouring out their heartaches to a fellow drinker or the bartender. They have hurts and needs, all right! We just need to learn how to communicate Jesus effectively with them.

The focus of the conversation never changes: Jesus. But we may need to adapt our conversation to what we know about the person we are speaking with.

For many of us who have been followers of Jesus for a while, one of the biggest obstacles is the churchy language we have picked up. "Atonement." "Redemption." "Washed in the blood." There's nothing wrong with such terms per se (indeed, many of them come right out of the Bible), but if we are using them with people who have no church background, they won't be able to follow what we are saying.

Generally, simple, plain, straightforward terms work the best. Jesus told parables about the things the people of His day understood—farming, fishing, and so on. Likewise, we should use ordinary, everyday language as we share about Him.

No matter how true what you are saying is, if others can't understand it, it is wasted.

- *Be yourself.* "The Son of Man has come eating and drinking, and you say, 'Look, a glutton and a winebibber, a friend of tax collectors and sinners!' " (Luke 7:34).

Jesus wasn't really a glutton or drunkard, of course, but He did enjoy having a good time—even if it was in the presence of some people who were not acceptable in the more pious circles. Jesus was no party pooper. He wanted to be with people and to minister among them, and He didn't let others' disapproval stop Him.

The lesson for us is that we shouldn't take ourselves so seriously that we can't smile, have fun, and act naturally. That's actually best for sharing Jesus with others.

Sometimes people, when it comes to speaking about spiritual things, will change their voice and personality, even their posture. Suddenly they are acting really "religious" and super spiritual, not their normal selves at all.

No! This is not the proper way to communicate. We should use the same voice in talking about Jesus as we do in talking about everyday subjects such as sports or shopping. And we should act the same way when speaking of spiritual things as we do at any other time. Anything else is unnatural or even hypocritical.

We all know that we can put on different personas if we want to. But ask yourself this: which is the best you? It's the person who you naturally are. Let this person be changed to reflect Christ (2 Corinthians 3:18), and then unbelievers will see Christ in you and be drawn to Him.

- *Show love to others.* "Though I speak with the tongues of men and of angels, but have not love, I have become sounding brass or a clanging cymbal" (1 Corinthians 13:1).

Once, in Africa, I was carrying the cross and speaking from village to village with the help of an interpreter. This interpreter would preach alongside me, delivering a powerful message about salvation in Jesus. But then, do you know what he would do when he was done preaching? Instead of mingling with the people, he would go and sit inside a car. Oh, this man cared a lot about winning "souls" for Jesus, but he didn't love *people.*

The people with whom we are sharing Jesus can tell whether or not we love them. That's why we need to be so full of the love of God that it oozes out of us. Our faces should shine with God's love. People are attracted to that. On the other hand, they will turn away from an unloving follower of Christ.

Ask yourself whether in fact you do love unbelievers, as God loves them. And should the answer be no, then deal with God about that. When you ask Him to help you love others more, He will do so.

Next, ask yourself whether you are displaying the love that you feel. In fact, try this experiment: Stand in front of a mirror and look at the expression on your face. Is it grim or joyful? Practice standing up straight, looking directly into your own eyes, and smiling in a friendly way.

That's how you should look as you are speaking to others about Jesus.

- *Let the method fit the place.* "To everything there is a season" (Ecclesiastes 3:1).

We may be sharing Jesus with the homeless in an alley, or we may be sharing at an elegant dinner party. We may be sharing with an old friend or with a stranger. We may have only a few seconds in a grocery store checkout line, or we may have an extended period to talk during a car trip. The situations where we can speak of our Savior are incredibly diverse, and so are the ways we can be sharing.

The apostle Paul said, "I have become all things to all men, that I might by all means save some" (1 Corinthians 9:22). Jesus sometimes preached to crowds and sometimes spoke in intimate settings, and He healed differently from occasion to occasion. Likewise, we can adapt ourselves to the situations we find ourselves in.

Should you be in a grocery store line, for example, you might not have enough time to do more than hand out a gospel tract. In another situation, you might do something else—that's all right. There's no bad way to witness, so long as you are sharing Jesus and His love. Don't worry about it. Just do your best at what you feel God is leading you to do in a given situation.

- *Lift up Jesus and lift people up to Him.* Jesus said, "I, if I am lifted up from the earth, will draw all peoples to Myself" (John 12:32).

Jesus was lifted up from the earth on the cross to bear the sins of us all. He is likewise "lifted up" when we praise and magnify Him. As people are presented with the image of the Savior, they are drawn to Him for salvation.

Our objective should always be to help people be lifted up to Christ. This means we should never put them down. Criticism and condemnation keep people from rising to put their hope and trust in Jesus.

- *Focus on Jesus, not the enemy.* "He who is in you is greater than he who is in the world" (1 John 4:4).

Sometimes when followers of Jesus are talking about spiritual things with unbelievers, they get drawn into talking about the problems in the world. In other words, they are focused on what our spiritual enemy, the devil, is doing. Meanwhile, they are not lifting up Jesus, the assured victor over the enemy.

Certainly there *is* spiritual darkness in the world. But we all know that already. So let's not dwell on it. Instead, let's show people the solution to the problems of the world: Jesus. In Him is the power to change lives and to change the world.

- *Don't let yourself be drawn into arguments.* "Avoid foolish and ignorant disputes, knowing that they generate strife" (2 Timothy 2:23).

Sometimes, when we are sharing Jesus with others, they will bring up a controversial subject, such as the role of Christians in politics, the failures of prominent church leaders, the dilemma of unmarried people living together, or any number of other topics. And when the subject is one we feel strongly about, we might be tempted to argue the point. But we have to resist that temptation. An argument like that isn't going to do anything to move the other person closer to Jesus.

All other subjects—as important as they might be to discuss within certain contexts—are secondary in comparison to the subject of Jesus Christ when we are speaking with someone who needs to be born again. So develop your skill at turning a conversation back to the subject of Jesus whenever it threatens to be diverted. Here are some examples to show you what I mean:

UNBELIEVER: "You're one of those people who refuse to believe in science, aren't you? Don't you know it's a proven fact that people evolved from lower life forms by natural processes?"

JESUS FOLLOWER: "We could get into a big debate about that. But what do you think about Jesus? What attracts you about Him?"

UNBELIEVER: "I used to go to church. They were all a bunch of hypocrites."

JESUS FOLLOWER: "Well, I can't defend them. I don't know them. But I know the greatest person in history—Jesus. You don't think He was a hypocrite, do you?"

UNBELIEVER: "Oh, you must be one of those fundamentalists. Why don't you people want to let us gays fall in love and get married just like you do?"

JESUS FOLLOWER: "I'm not here to talk about gay marriage. I do know that as we receive Christ and begin studying the Bible, God gives us light about all sorts of issues."

This is an area where working as a team can really help. For example, if two believers are talking with two unbelievers and one of the unbelievers is becoming argumentative and mocking, the believers could gently try to separate the unbelievers. That way, one of the believers could focus on sharing with the person who seems more responsive.

Nevertheless, there may be times when, no matter how hard we try to turn the conversation back to Jesus, a person will insist on talking about whatever hot-button issue is on his or her mind. At that point the conversation is going to be nothing but counterproductive. We need to exit from it in a gracious way, saying something like "God bless you. I will pray for you."

Most of the time, however, I have found that people are willing to discuss Jesus as we nudge them in that direction. The key is for us not to let ourselves get bogged down in issues of theology or morality. We are not out to persuade someone of our own beliefs. The claims of Jesus are what matter. He is the one who will bring people to a point of life change.

- *Don't try to "fix" others.* "Each one shall bear his own load" (Galatians 6:5).

I have seen it time and time again. A follower of Jesus will share the good news of salvation with a person, and the other will accept Christ. Hallelujah! But then they will get to talking about the problems in the new believer's life. "My husband left me." "I don't have a job." "I'm depressed and I've been feeling suicidal."

Then the mature follower of Jesus—with the best intentions in the world—will start to get involved in the other's life. Go over to the new believer's house. Offer advice. Spend long periods of time trying to deal with the problem issues.

Before they know it, the mature believer has gotten bogged down in helping the other person. Often he is doing no good, or is even being counterproductive, because he has gotten involved in areas that he knows little about. Meanwhile, he is no longer sharing Jesus with other people who need to know Him. Sometimes emotional entanglement will even lead to a sinful relationship.

This piece of advice might sound harsh, but trust me, it is for the best: beware of getting too involved in another's life. You are not the Savior. Let the real Savior, Jesus, bring healing to another's life. Assuming you are not a trained marriage counselor, for example, you shouldn't be trying to reconcile an estranged couple. Don't get into an area you don't know much about.

~

...remember that you can't fix every problem in someone else's life.

~

I'm not saying that you should not disciple a new believer (see chapter eight). By all means, pray with people and point them to what the Bible says about their problems. But remember that you can't fix every problem in someone else's life. Entrust them to Jesus; He is more than capable of taking care of their needs.

- *Don't worry about failure.* "Well done, good and faithful servant" (Matthew 25:21).

Some think that if someone with whom they have shared Jesus does not decide on the spot to trust in Him, then they have failed. But that's wrong. There is no "failure" in sharing Jesus. As long as we have faithfully told someone about Jesus, we have been a success, regardless of how the other has responded.

What a relief! When we think that we must win someone to Christ, we are under tremendous pressure and then feel defeated when someone rejects Him. We might be tempted to quit sharing Jesus. Or we might become so pushy that we turn people off. But when we realize that we can do nothing to save someone, that only God can do that, it takes all the pressure off.

Don't get me wrong: every time we share Jesus with someone, our objective should be to win that person to Christ then and there. At the same time, however, we must realize that it doesn't always work that way. Sometimes we sow; sometimes we water; sometimes we harvest.

Even Jesus met rejection when He ministered to people face to face. Do we really think we will never see rejection when we tell others about Him?

Our reaction when someone chooses not to respond to Jesus' invitation should be to say, "God bless you," and then to pray for their eventual salvation. We don't need to be discouraged, because we realize that the seeds we have planted might yet bear fruit.

It's all about Jesus. The kingdom belongs to Him. He will usher people in when and how He chooses.

THE GREATEST CHALLENGE

I could go on giving communication tips, but I think the ones I have included above cover most of the common areas of difficulty. Certainly, as you have discovered an area where you could improve, it should energize you, not discourage you. Now you can get better at sharing the Lord of the universe with those who need to know Him!

Have you ever been to the lighting section of one of those vast home supply stores? How many different lampshades did you see there? There are dark ones, light ones, formal ones, funky ones; all different colors, sizes, and shapes. Believe it or not, there are people who spend their entire careers coming up with lampshades to appeal to every possible taste among the lampshade-buying public.

The prospect before us is something like designing different lampshades. Throughout the course of our "career" of sharing Jesus, we may need to learn to share Jesus with people of many different cultures, religions, social statuses, education levels, and so on. But we're not just selling something to diffuse the light from a light bulb; we are sharing the chance to know the Son of God and Savior!

After a lifetime of sharing Jesus, we should be much better at it than when we started. But whether we are or not, that shouldn't keep us from doing what we can now.

We don't have to worry that we aren't as good at it now as we will be in, say, twenty years' time. Although we have a lifetime of learning ahead of us, we can start where we are. God will bless and use us where we are this year, next year, and for the rest of our lives.

∾ ∾ ∾

QUESTIONS TO CONSIDER

• How would you rate your ability to communicate about Jesus effectively with the people you meet?

• Look back through the list of communication tips. Which two or three do you want to work on the most?

10

HANDLING DOUBTS AND QUESTIONS

Sanctify the Lord God in your hearts, and always be ready to give a defense to everyone who asks you a reason for the hope that is in you.

—1 Peter 3:15

A pastor friend of mine would ask me to preach at his church from time to time. And every time I showed up at his church, I could see that more atheists and agnostics and out-and-out sinners had gotten saved and were worshiping Jesus as part of this church.

So one time I asked my friend, "How do you lead so many atheists to Jesus?"

He said, "I send out our new converts to the homes of the worst people in town."

"Not your deacons? Not your elders? Not the leaders of the church?"

"Oh no. They would try to convince the unbelievers about what they need to do. I send out new converts, and the only thing they know is Jesus. So they get to the people's house and the unbelievers will start saying, 'Well, I don't believe in God. I believe in this and I believe in that.' And the new followers of Jesus will say, 'I don't know anything about that. All I know is that two weeks ago Jesus convicted me of my sin, and He saved me and now I'm a new man.' The unbelievers will start crying, and their tears just wash them into the kingdom of God."

I tell this story to make the point that *any* follower of Jesus can share Him effectively with others, regardless of what issues the others may raise. You don't have to be an expert in any area of belief, and you don't have to fear anyone's questions, because you're going to keep the subject focused on Jesus anyway. As a follower of His, you are fully qualified to represent Him. All you have to do is tell what you know about Him.

WITNESSES, NOT DEBATERS

One thing that scares many people off from sharing Jesus with others is their fear that someone will raise a question or objection that they don't know how to deal with. To that, as my Aussie friends say, no worries!

It's true that the apostle Peter urged, "Sanctify the Lord God in your hearts, and always be ready to give a defense to everyone who asks you a reason for the hope that is in you" (1 Peter 3:15). And many take that to mean that they have to study up so that they know answers to all kinds of difficult questions. But look at the verse more carefully. It simply says that we should be spiritually right with God (the Lord sanctified in our hearts) and be prepared to tell people our story about why we believe in the Lord (the hope that is in us).

~

We're not in the answering-questions business; we're in the sharing-Jesus business.

~

We may or may not have an answer to someone's question. But when we don't, that's all right, because we don't need to. We're not in the answering-questions business; we're in the sharing-Jesus business. Whatever doubts or questions someone may have, our goal is to direct that person back to Jesus as swiftly as possible. He is the answer to all questions.

Now, I know that the normal rules of being a good listener tell us that we should let people say whatever they want. But I have found that this is not necessarily the best way to share Jesus. Sometimes people want to divert the conversation. When we start talking about Jesus, they will ask us where Cain got his wife or express their views on abortion or tell us why they got mad and left the church twenty years ago. But we don't have to let the other person dictate the course of the conversation.

Many times, when someone has gone off on a tangent, I will say, "I know what you're saying there, but let me ask you this. What about Jesus? Do you think He would make a difference in that situation?" In other words, I take back control of the conversation and put the focus squarely back on Jesus.

When Jesus walked this earth, people came to Him with all kinds of questions, trying to trap Him instead of really searching for the truth they needed to embrace. Did Jesus let them get away with that? Certainly not. He said what He wanted to say—what needed to be said in each situation. In His name, we can do the same. And really, it's the compassionate thing to do for the other persons, since we're trying to keep them on the path to the solution for their main problem: sin.

The apostle Paul once wrote, "I determined not to know anything among you except Jesus Christ and Him crucified" (1 Corinthians 2:2). That should be our intention as well. Even if we think we have a great comeback for somebody's objection, we should not necessarily trot it out. We are called to be witnesses to Christ, not debaters.

In case taking control of a conversation should seem hard to you, let me remind you that we are to be sharing Jesus in the power of the Spirit. That applies to responding to people's doubts and questions as well as to every other part of the sharing. The Holy Spirit will lead us so that we know what to say in response to someone's questions and know how to introduce that person to Jesus.

People sometimes talk about me as being a great "soul winner." I'm not. As a matter of fact, I couldn't do anything to change anyone's heart if I tried. I just keep offering Jesus, and He does it all. I'm merely around to play a helping role and to watch what God is doing and give Him praise. Glory, hallelujah!

My advice to you is to do the same. Stay where the anointing is. Stick with Jesus.

READY RESPONSES

As we are sharing Jesus with people, inevitably some will express doubts or raise questions. I would like to share with you some of these that I have found to be most common, along with ready responses for each.

• *"I'm not ready."* "Today, if you will hear His voice, do not harden your hearts" (Hebrews 3:15).

"I'm not ready" is an objection that we simply cannot accept. When someone says that to me, I respond, "You may not be *willing*, but you are *ready*. You need Jesus, and He's calling out to you today. There's no reason why you cannot receive Him right now."

When that's not enough to encourage someone to pray for salvation, I try another tack. I'll ask, "Do you feel good right now?"

"Yes, I feel fine."

"Do you think you're sick?"

"No, I said I feel fine. There's nothing wrong with me."

"Okay, now let me ask you something else. Imagine that you went to the doctor today for a checkup and, after running his tests, he said, 'You've got a disease and you're about to die.' How would you feel then?"

"Well, I'd be concerned."

"Right. Because you got the doctor's report that you've got a real problem.

"The Bible tells us what our real problem is, spiritually. It's spelled s-i-n, and it's eating away at you. One day, if left untreated, it's going to kill you and separate you from God. That's why Jesus died for you—to save you from that outcome.

"Now, with this new information, are you ready to see Dr. Jesus?"

- *"I'm too sinful."* "Though your sins are like scarlet, they shall be as white as snow" (Isaiah 1:18).

While some people have too weak a sense of their own sinfulness, others are so acutely aware of their sin that they think they are beyond God's forgiveness. We can help them understand that God forgives anyone who trusts in His Son, Jesus. All of us can be forgiven, no matter what we have done.

The Bible is full of stories about people who did terrible things and yet were accepted by God because they repented and turned to Him. Moses murdered a man (Exodus 2:12). David committed both adultery and murder (2 Samuel 11:2-4, 14-17). The apostle Paul persecuted the early church (Acts 22:4).

The author of the famous hymn "Amazing Grace" was a former slave ship captain named John Newton. He certainly needed grace, after what he had done to his African victims. And indeed there is amazing grace for every sinner who comes to God in humility. The only unforgivable sin is "blasphemy against the Spirit" (Matthew 12:31), which is rejecting the salvation God offers in Jesus. All who desire salvation can have it.

- *"I like to have fun."* "There is joy in the presence of the angels of God over one sinner who repents" (Luke 15:10).

A number of people have the mistaken notion that being a follower of Jesus is a dreary business. They don't want to exchange the "fun" of running their own lives— whether they are into taking drugs or sleeping around or whatever—for what they perceive as the grim life of a Jesus follower.

The problem is, these people don't really understand fun.

Sin offers its "passing pleasures," to be sure (Hebrews 11:25). But that kind of pleasure has a hollowness or joy-lessness because it exists apart from the life God intended for us to have. It is haunted by a sense of *Is this all there is?* or s*omething's not right about this.*

True fun—real joy—comes in following Jesus. "Believing, you rejoice with joy inexpressible and full of glory" (1 Peter 1:8). Only in Jesus can we be put into right relationships with our Maker, with ourselves, and with the other people in our lives, thus making true happiness possible.

Jesus' tale about the prodigal son in Luke 15:11-32 describes the father in the story (representing God) as putting on a wonderful party when his son (representing a repentant sinner) comes home. So we need to let people who say they are having too much fun to follow Jesus know that when they are saved they can rejoice on earth at the same time that angels are rejoicing over them in heaven. Now, *that's* a party!

- *"The church is full of hypocrites."* "All the nations will be gathered before [the Son of Man], and He will separate them one from another, as a shepherd divides his sheep from the goats" (Matthew 25:32).

The complaint about hypocrites is a common one and is truer than I'm sure any of us would like to admit. And it should make us examine ourselves as to whether we are following Jesus in as truthful and consistent a manner as we could. Still, the presence of hypocrites should in no way prevent someone from choosing to follow Jesus.

~

No one stops going to movies or ball games because of hypocrites in the seats.

~

Hypocrites are everywhere. But no one stops eating at restaurants because there are hypocrites there. No one stops going to movies or ball games because of hypocrites in the seats. And likewise, no one should hesitate about coming into the kingdom of God just because he or she might run up against some hypocrites.

Jesus criticized hypocrisy more powerfully than any of us could (see, for example, Matthew 23:25-28). And one day Jesus, as the Judge of all humanity, will separate out His true followers from all the rest. Perfect justice will be done on that day. In the meantime, though, we have to accept that hypocrisy exists—even within ourselves.

Sometimes, when I am speaking with an unbeliever who is complaining about hypocrites, I ask him, "What do you think that people who are completely unhypo-critical would look like? How would they live? How would they act?"

I listen patiently while the other person gives me his opinion about a hypocrisy-free lifestyle.

Afterward, I follow up with "And does that describe your life?"

"Um ... well, no." His own words have condemned him.

At that point I laugh and say something like "Yeah, we all need the grace of God, don't we? Let's get back to talking about how you can give your heart to Jesus."

- *"How could God let bad things happen?"* "Oh, the depth of the riches both of the wisdom and knowl-edge of God! How unsearchable are His judgments and His ways past finding out!" (Romans 11:33).

Many people wonder how bad things can happen if God is good and has unlimited power. The answer is, we don't know. We're not God. He's greater and wiser than we are (hallelujah for that!). He is in charge, so we just need to trust Him, even when we don't understand everything.

I was talking about Jesus with an ex-Marine on a beach in Florida when he began acting bitter toward God.

"What's bothering you?" I asked.

"I was in Beirut in October 1983 when that bomb blew up at the Marine barracks and 241 Marines, sailors, and soldiers were killed," he said. "I was in those barracks, and many of my friends were killed. How could God allow that to happen?"

I looked him in the eye and said, "I don't know. I don't understand it any more than you do."

Then I let him know that I understood his frustration at not knowing. "I have a handicapped son," I said. "I've prayed over him. I took him to Jerusalem and laid him on the rocks at the Mount of Olives. I've done everything I know to do for him. But God has chosen to let him remain handicapped."

Joseph is now thirty years old and still wears diapers.

"I don't understand all the reasons," I told the bitter ex-Marine, "but I know that my son is the way God made him. And I trust Him."

The Marine began to cry and gave his heart to Jesus that day.

The problem of evil in the world is one area where we shouldn't even try to answer the question, since we don't have the whole answer. It's better to admit the perplexity of the situation, comfort people in their hurting, and point them to Jesus, whose suffering on our behalf was greater than anything we will ever undergo.

- *"There are many ways to God."* "Jesus said to [Thomas], 'I am the way, the truth, and the life. No one comes to the Father except through Me' " (John 14:6).

Here's a frequent objection these days. It seems that nearly everyone today believes that you can get to God by following the Hindu way, the Muslim way, the Christian way, or any home-brewed combination of spiritual beliefs you like. And it sounds so tolerant, doesn't it? —So friendly toward people of all persuasions.

It is also a lie that prevents people from coming to God at all.

We can't bend on this point. We can't agree that there are many ways to God, for if we did, there would be no point in following Jesus or sharing Him with others. It's just not true that every religious and spiritual belief is as good as every other. Jesus is *the* way to God—the only way. (We will get into this in more depth in the chapter to follow.)

At the same time, we don't want to antagonize another person unnecessarily. We should emphasize the goodness of God in providing a means for salvation in His Son, not criticize other beliefs. We just want the other person to consider (perhaps for the first time) the exclusive claim of Jesus. Should the unbeliever not like that, then he has a problem with Jesus, not with us. We're just quoting His words.

- *"I don't believe in the Bible."* "The word of God is living, and powerful, and sharper than any two-edged sword, piercing even to the division of soul and spirit, and of the joints and marrow, and is a discerner of the thoughts and intents of the heart" (Hebrews 4:12).

We love the Bible and rightly believe that it comes from God as His trustworthy guide for our lives. And that's what makes it hard for us when others disrespect the Bible and maybe start picking on some Bible story they find hard to swallow, such as Creation, the Flood, Jonah's big fish, or whatever else it might be.

But just as with every other issue, we have to avoid being drawn into a discussion on this secondary point so that we can focus on Jesus—the number-one priority. Besides, the Bible doesn't need our defense. When others come to know Jesus, the Holy Spirit will begin developing in them a proper respect for Holy Scripture.

Let me share with you a strategy that has worked for me. When someone says, "I don't believe the Bible," I quote John 3:16: "God so loved the world that He gave His only begotten Son, that whoever believes in Him should not perish but have everlasting life." Then I ask, "What don't you believe about that?"

You see, this strategy uses the Bible, which is the issue that the other person has raised. And we believe that God honors His Word. But we're not debating or arguing with the other person. We're putting his or her focus back on Jesus and trusting God to draw the unbeliever to Him through His Word.

- *"I was born a Christian."* "As many as received [Christ], to them He gave the right to become children of God, to those who believe in His name: who were born, not of blood, nor of the will of the flesh, nor of the will of man, but of God" (John 1:12-13).

People have all kinds of misconceptions about what it means to follow Jesus. One of the most common is expressed by the comment "I was born a Christian." When you hear this one, you know you are dealing with someone whose birth family self-identified as Christians and who probably has gone to church at least a little. You also know that you are dealing with someone who really doesn't get what it means to know Jesus!

Growing up in a family where Jesus is loved and obeyed is a great blessing. I will forever be grateful for the example of faithfulness to Jesus that I had in my own dear mother. But still, the new life in Jesus is not like our eye color or the shape of our nose. We don't inherit it from our parents any more than we get it by going to church, agreeing with certain doctrines, or following religious rituals.

When people say, "I was born a Christian," we need to explain to them that new life in Jesus is a gift from God that comes to us when we personally and individually choose to believe in Jesus. As this opens their eyes to a need they didn't even know they had, we can encourage them to take the step of trusting in Jesus for themselves.

- *"I don't believe in God."* "The fool has said in his heart, 'There is no God' " (Psalm 14:1).

The majority of people—at least in most countries—have *some* kind of belief in God or a god or some gods. But every once in a while you will run up against someone who says, "I don't believe in God. I'm an atheist."

Most of the time, in a situation like that, I tap the self-proclaimed atheist on the shoulder, laugh, and say, "You're smarter than that." And then I go on talking about Jesus and His offer of new life.

But if the other person insists that there is no God, I get more profound. I say, "Look at this watch on my arm."

When the other person has noticed my watch, I continue, "It just happened there."

The atheist says, "What?"

"It just happened there. One day, as I was walking along, it just appeared there on my arm."

"Come on. Somebody put it there—you did or somebody else did."

I say, "It's a great watch—keeps perfect time—but nobody put it there. It just evolved on my arm."

And then I give up the pretense. "No. You know what this watch is? This watch is a reflection of creativity and power. Somebody had the design in his mind. Somebody had the creativity to design it. Somebody had the power to make it. That's what this watch is."

The atheist has to admit, "Yeah, that's true."

Then I say, "But what about the arm that the watch is on? My arm is far more complicated than this watch. This arm and the rest of me are a reflection of the design, the creativity, and the power of God."

Most of the time, at this juncture, the atheist has gotten the point and we can go on to discuss what the cross of Jesus can do for him.

- *"I'm mad at God."* "A soft answer turns away wrath, but a harsh word stirs up anger" (Proverbs 15:1).

Sometimes, when we start talking about Jesus, the other person will get upset and start spewing angry words. Maybe this person has had a bad experience with self-professed followers of Jesus before. Many times, though, he or she may be angry, not at us, but at God. In either case, we should not take the anger personally.

One time I met a woman on a street, handed her a "Smile, God loves you" sticker and said, "God loves you" to her. That seems inoffensive enough, doesn't it? Well, she started screaming at me. I waited for her to calm down a bit and then said, "Ma'am, I can see that you're hurting."

She replied, "Yes. Last week a car ran over my child and killed it. How could God let that happen?"

This woman had a good reason for feeling hurt. I could only feel compassion for her and minister to her in the best way I knew how.

People can become angry at God for any number of reasons. They have had disappointments, loss, or pain, and they blame God for it. We, by sharing Jesus with them, unfortunately wind up taking some of the heat of their anger. But they're really not angry with us—they're angry with God. That's why we can't take it personally or get offended or become angry in return. We must respond to a harsh word with a soft answer.

When someone is really angry, it takes a judgment call on our part as to whether we ought to even continue trying to share Jesus. One time the citizens of Nazareth got so angry at Jesus that they took Him to a cliff, intending to toss Him over it and kill Him. What did Jesus do? "Passing through the midst of them, He went His way" (Luke 4:30). Sometimes we must do the same.

- *"I don't like religion."* "If anyone among you thinks he is religious, and does not bridle his tongue but deceives his own heart, this one's religion is useless" (James 1:26).

I have sympathy for people who say they don't like religion—I don't like it myself. Wars have been fought over religion. Terrorist acts are justified with religion. Injustice and oppression of every type are commonly based in religion. Who wants that?

$\sim$

I'm there to share with them about a person— Jesus...

$\sim$

As James 1 says, religion is useless when the heart is not right. So when people say they don't like religion, I tell them that I agree with them and that I'm not peddling religion. I'm there to share with them about a person— Jesus—and not try to induct them into some religious system.

I find that people respond much better to Jesus than they do to religion. And well they should. And so we need to focus, not on the institution of Christianity, but on Christ as the One who can change hearts and lives.

- *"I don't have enough faith."* "If you have faith as a mustard seed, you will say to this mountain, 'Move from here to there,' and it will move; and nothing will be impossible for you" (Matthew 17:20).

I'm not sure why people say, "I don't have enough faith," but I hear it from time to time. Maybe it comes from genuine humility—and that's not a bad thing. But when someone says this, we want to prevent it from becoming an excuse to delay putting trust in Jesus.

Keeping in mind Jesus' words about faith as a mustard seed, I will often say to a person, "Do you have even a tiny bit of faith?"

She might say, "Well, yeah, I have a tiny bit. But compared to people like you who have a big faith, I hardly have any."

"Great! That's all you need."

"Really?"

That's when I stick out my hand and say, "Now, I want you to imagine that this is the hand of Jesus and you're saying to Him, 'I only have a tiny grain of faith in You, Jesus, but I'm putting it in Your hand.' "

I encourage the other person to pretend to put a small kernel of grain into my palm. (Sometimes she will start crying right then!) Then I say, "The Bible tells us that faith is a gift of God. So let's ask God to work a miracle and grow your tiny grain into a great big faith." And I pray, 'Lord, take this little mustard seed of faith and multiply it so that this dear woman can be saved.' "

Often, at that point, the other person's heart has softened and she has begun to hope as she never has before. Then I can immediately lead her into a prayer asking Jesus into her heart.

The key here, as with every other expressed doubt or question, is to deal with the objection simply and honestly while trying to move the conversation as quickly as possible back to Jesus and His offer of new life. Remembering that it's all about Jesus, we try to introduce people to the Savior, who can then set about dealing with whatever problems or concerns they might have.

∽∽∽

QUESTIONS TO CONSIDER

- What doubts or questions about Jesus have others raised with you in the past? How have you handled them?

- What could you change in your approach to more effectively keep the focus of a discussion on Jesus?

11

JESUS AND THE WORLD'S RELIGIONS

There is one God and one Mediator between God and men, the Man Christ Jesus, who gave Himself a ransom for all.

—1 Timothy 2:5-6

One day I was talking with my wife, Denise, and some others about sharing Jesus with people of different religions. After several minutes, Denise said, "Arthur, no matter who you're talking to and what religion they belong to, you have the same response for them: Jesus."

I said, "That's right! It's all about Jesus."

And it's true. In one sense, it doesn't matter what religion a person identifies with. Every single one of us on the globe, regardless of religious involvement (or lack thereof), needs Jesus. That makes sharing with different people a lot simpler!

I know what I'm talking about here. During my cross walk around the world, I have shared Jesus with people who live in every nation of the world and who belong to all of the world's major religions. I have also seen thousands of them receive Jesus as Savior and Lord and become followers of Jesus.

A LIFE GIVEN, BLOOD SHED, A COVERING MADE

Comparative religions experts like to show how different religions resemble each other. But there is one important—indeed, crucial—way in which following Jesus is different from practicing any other religion.

In almost all religions, people are trying to make contact with God through some kind of self-effort. The followers of Jesus have a totally different concept. The Bible teaches us that God first loved us and that He reaches out to us. Salvation, then, lies not in our own efforts but instead was provided through Jesus' death on the cross. We need only to repent and receive Jesus as our Savior and Lord.

Now, I say all this not to put down other religions. In fact, we should *never* put down or make fun of other religions. But I want to make very clear that the cross is an absolute necessity for anyone to be accepted by God. Self-effort, however well intended, will never bring anyone into the kingdom of God; only receiving salvation as a gift because of the blood of Christ can do that.

The Bible is consistent all the way through in demonstrating that the shedding of blood is essential to forgiveness. The Old Testament law teaches that "the life of all flesh is its blood" (Leviticus 17:14). Referring to Jesus' self-sacrifice, the writer to the Hebrews said, "Without shedding of blood is no remission [of sin]" (Hebrews 9:22).

The importance of death and blood goes right back to the first sin. After Adam and Eve had transgressed against God, but before He cast them out of the Garden of Eden, God used animal skin to make clothes for the first couple (Genesis 3:21). In other words, He killed one or more animals to make this covering possible for them.

Several laws and incidents from the Old Testament period reveal the importance of blood in deliverance from sin. Abraham led his son Isaac up a mountain and laid him upon an altar at the command of God, but God then provided a ram to take Isaac's place. God told Moses that the Hebrews in Egypt were to put the blood of lambs upon their doorposts so that when the death angel came, he would see the blood and pass by. Once a year the high priest was to kill a spotless lamb and sprinkle its blood upon the altar in the holy of holies.

But all this was preparatory for the paramount case of blood shedding in history: the sacrifice of Jesus.

Jesus was born without sin. The Holy Spirit put the seed of Jesus in His mother's womb. And we know that the blood of the mother does not run through the child. The child receives nourishment from the mother but not the blood of the mother. So the blood of Jesus was the holy blood of God.

Jesus lived without sin. He showed His power over all the created universe as He healed the sick, raised the dead, controlled the weather, walked on water, multiplied bread and fish, and did many other miraculous things, including raising the dead. Then Jesus, fulfilling the prophecies of the Scriptures, suffered, carried the cross, and was crucified on the cross for our sins.

In many places, the Scriptures tell us about the effectiveness of Jesus' blood in washing away our sin. Jesus Himself, when celebrating Passover with His disciples on the night before His death, declared, "This is My blood of the new covenant, which is shed for many for the remission of sins" (Matthew 26:28).

~

As we think about the religions of the world, we must always remember that salvation is not by the works of a person but by the cleansing blood of Jesus.

~

We are also told, "Jesus Christ ... loved us and washed us from our sins in His own blood" (Revelation 1:5). That's what soap does with dirt and stains. It loosens the dirt from the cloth so that the water washes it away. Jesus loosens the sin from us and washes it away in His blood.

As we think about the religions of the world, we must always remember that salvation is not by the works of a person but by the cleansing blood of Jesus. "Nor is there salvation in any other, for there is no other name under heaven given among men by which we must be saved" (Acts 4:12). And in the end, all people will recognize the supremacy of Jesus.

> *God also has highly exalted Him and given Him the name which is above every name, that at the name of Jesus every knee should bow, of those in heaven, and of those on earth, and of those under the earth, and that every tongue should confess that Jesus Christ is Lord, to the glory of God the Father.* (Philippians 2:9-11)

Let us obey Christ the Lord and share the loving message and person of Jesus with the world. There is hope, love, mercy, and salvation for all who call upon the name of the Lord. Remember, Jesus gave His life; Jesus shed His blood; Jesus is the covering for our sins.

JESUS FOR ALL

The following are tips for sharing Jesus with people of other religions or none. Remember, the most important thing is always to stay with the subject of Jesus.

- *Islam.* Jesus said, "Blessed are the pure in heart, for they shall see God" (Matthew 5:8).

Muslims believe in a personal god. As is true of all religions, one of the most powerful points in sharing with a Muslim is how we can have a pure heart.

I will often ask a Muslim, "How do you have a pure heart?"

He will then tell me how he obeys the rules of his religion, gives alms, and so on.

Then I say, "I don't know about you, but my efforts and goodness don't take away any sins of mine, nor do they give me a pure heart. What I need is a new heart and a new life, and that's what Jesus came to give. 'If anyone is in Christ, he is a new creation.' Jesus will give this new heart and new life and make a home for us in heaven."

At other times, I'll just start talking about Jesus. After all, Jesus is mentioned in the Qur'an and is honored within Islam, which considers Him to be a prophet but not the Son of God. I will say, "I don't know much about Muhammad, so let's talk about Jesus." And we do.

On one occasion my wife, Denise, and I were climbing the mountains of Hindu Cush with the cross, going from Pakistan into Afghanistan. We got as high as 18,200 feet above sea level, high above two glaciers, and carried the cross from village to village. Meanwhile, our guide was a Muslim who at first refused to interpret for us the message of Jesus. In fact, he refused to even say the name of Jesus. But God was healing people, and we would communicate with the people using simple hand signals, such as pointing to someone's heart and saying, "Jesus."

Our guide watched what was going on and finally was willing to discuss the life and message of Jesus with us. Before we left that part of the world, he came to believe in and receive Jesus Christ as his Savior and Lord. He has since gone back to those villages, sharing the message of Jesus, and many have become followers of Jesus.

Here is an e-mail message that I received from him recently:

> Thanks to my Lord and for your guidance. This is you and your patronage and prayers. I can see the big change in my life. I am feeling proud. My Lord Jesus is coming to me in dreams. He is so happy. I am so happy. Sometimes I see Him in the day while walking on the road traveling, and sometimes in the office. Yes, every movement and every time when I used to do some good works. Oh my Lord Jesus I love You. I praise. I praise You. I thank You. You are my protector. You're my only provider. My praise and love is for You.

- *Judaism.* "Let all the house of Israel know assuredly that God has made this Jesus, whom you crucified, both Lord and Christ" (Acts 2:36).

Jews believe in a personal God, the God of the Hebrews Scriptures (Old Testament). And Jesus was a Jew. But Jews are like everybody else in the world in that they need Jesus as Savior and Lord. I find that most Jewish people are interested in hearing about Jesus and His message.

In 1980, political relations between Israel and Egypt improved as the two countries exchanged ambassadors and recognized each other. The border between the two nations was scheduled to be opened so that travelers could pass from one nation to the other. I was called by Jesus to carry the cross from Jerusalem to Cairo across the Sinai Desert and to be the first person allowed through on the historic day when the border opened.

The day before the border opening, I walked up to the Israeli side of the border and spoke to the captain standing there. I said, "I want to be first in line tomorrow. Where does the line form, so I can put my sleeping bag there?"

He said, "Well, you'll be first. You've walked from Jerusalem."

I said, "But can I sleep here? I really want to be first."

He patted the gun on his hip and said, "I'm telling you, you'll be first in the morning. Do you really want to sleep here?"

I said, "That's fine with me."

"Wouldn't you like a bed?"

"Well, sure. I'd be willing, but I want to be first."

"I told you that you'll be first."

The captain went away to try and find someplace where I could spend the night. When he came back, the other officers were laughing and grinning and said to me, "Guess where you're spending the night tonight?"

"Where?"

"Prime Minister Begin's house."

They weren't kidding. Menachem Begin had a house in the Sinai, and I was invited to spend the night there. That night I stored my cross in the Israeli prime minister's living room.

The next morning I was back, first in line, and the same captain was standing there. I had learned his name was David Yaniv. I said, "Captain David, Jesus loves you. You can know Him."

He said, "Well, I'm Jewish."

I said, "Jesus was too, and He loves you. He died and rose again for you."

Maybe Yaniv had grown uncomfortable with the course of the conversation, because he changed the subject. He said, "They'll kill you over there. Those Muslims will kill you over in Egypt."

I replied, "They told me *you* were the bad guys."

"No, no. We're the good guys; *they're* the bad guys."

"One day you're going to get saved and worship Jesus."

Twenty-five years later, I appeared on a TBN television program, and guess who was on the set with me? David Yaniv. The Israeli captain who guarded that border is now a follower of Jesus and is the pastor of Roots Messianic Congregation in Lynnwood, Washington.

- *Hinduism.* "It is appointed for men to die once, but after this the judgment" (Hebrews 9:27).

This is an incredibly diverse and complex religion, with many gods and many religious practices. And because Hindus worship many gods, it is often no trouble getting them to accept Jesus as yet another god. The challenge is getting them to understand and accept the exclusive claims of Jesus and see their need of a personal Savior.

When sharing Jesus with a Hindu, we need to make very sure that our terms are clear and that we are communicating accurately.

One time Denise and I arrived in the nation of Myanmar and shared Jesus with our Hindu taxi driver. I thought we had done a great job of sharing about salvation in Jesus. Then, at the end of the conversation, I asked the driver, "Will you pray to receive Jesus?"

I was delighted to hear him say yes, and I started leading him in prayer. As I was finishing up the prayer, I used the phrase "and make my home in heaven."

At that point the taxi driver stopped repeating after me. He said, "I don't want to come back in heaven; I want to come back as an American."

I have to confess, that was one I didn't have a quick comeback for! But I quickly realized that the driver was thinking in reincarnation terms. I told him, "You have never been to America. America is not heaven." Then I tried to straighten out his thinking.

~

The resurrection of Jesus Christ makes all the difference in the world, perhaps especially with Hindus.

~

Another time, when talking to a Hindu in Bali, Indonesia, I handled it better. In sharing there with a man about Jesus, I went through the life of Jesus and the cross and the resurrection of Jesus. At that point the man interrupted and said, "Jesus was reincarnated. I can understand that."

"Listen carefully," I replied. "*Jesus came back in the same body.*"

The resurrection of Jesus Christ makes all the difference in the world, perhaps especially with Hindus. The risen Christ is not one of many gods but the unique God. This is what we have to help Hindus understand.

- *Buddhism.* "Men of Athens, I perceive that in all things you are very religious; for as I was passing through and considering the objects of your worship, I even found an altar with this inscription: TO THE UNKNOWN GOD. Therefore, the One whom you worship without knowing, Him I proclaim to you" (Acts 17:22-23).

Buddhists believe that God is a concept, not a personal Being. They remind me of some people whom the apostle Paul encountered in Athens. These Athenians had erected an altar inscribed "TO THE UNKNOWN GOD," and similarly Buddhists don't know God or even recognize that He exists. Paul said to the Athenians, "The One whom you worship without knowing, Him I proclaim to you" (Acts 17:23). Following his lead, we need to proclaim to Buddhists the God whom they are missing out on. We come to know God through His Son, Jesus.

Buddhism is about overcoming suffering. We can show what Jesus did to suffer for us and take away our need to suffer for our sins now and in eternity.

My wife, Denise, and I were carrying the cross in Sri Lanka—a predominately Buddhist nation—when one day a man came up to Denise and said, "What is his name?" He was pointing at me and at the cross.

Denise replied, "His name is Arthur Blessitt, and he is carrying the cross around the world."

The man said, "I've seen this," again pointing at the cross and me. "I was dying one night, but a Man came to me. Oh, I can never forget Him! He said I should follow Him. Afterward, I was immediately well.

"I began praying only to Him, but I did not know His name. Passing a store one day, I saw a picture of Him. He was hanging on a big cross like this. I said, 'This is the gentleman!' I bought the picture and follow only Him, but I don't know his name."

We explained to the man that I was not Jesus. This man did not even know the name of Jesus. So I told him that my name was Arthur Blessitt and that the man on the cross was Jesus.

We told him about the Bible, which explains much more about Jesus. We helped the man to understand who Jesus is from the Bible and know how to receive Him as Savior and Lord. We prayed with this man, and he gloriously welcomed Jesus into his life. It was one of the most moving times of witness I have ever experienced. Jesus had revealed Himself to this man; now we were privileged to tell him more and lead him into the Kingdom.

With Buddhists, like this man in Sri Lanka, it is important to show the need for a personal relationship with a personal God.

- *Jehovah's Witnesses and Mormons.* "I testify to every-one who hears the words of the prophecy of this book: If anyone adds to these things, God will add to him the plagues that are written in this book; and if anyone takes away from the words of the book of this prophecy, God shall take away his part from the Book of Life, from the holy city, and *from* the things which are written in this book" (Revelation 22:18-19).

These groups promote grave errors on the deity and person of Jesus, among other things. They have changed the Scriptures to reflect their false beliefs. We need to lead them to Jesus, the unique Son of God.

It is necessary for us to lead, and not be led by, those who come to our door seeking to convert us to Mormonism or the Jehovah's Witnesses. Sometimes, after giving a clear witness to them, we can then have a prayer with our visitors and say goodbye. We should never get caught up in arguing and debating about the Bible with them.

- *New Age.* "Beware of false prophets, who come to you in sheep's clothing, but inwardly they are raven-ous wolves" (Matthew 7:15).

New Agers are just grooving and wanting everybody to feel good about everything no matter what they are into. As they say in California, "different strokes for dif-ferent folks." With New Agers, we must point to the real-ity of sin and the personal need for Jesus.

- *Christian.* "I say to you, unless one is born again, he cannot see the kingdom of God" (John 3:3).

Not every Christian knows Jesus as Savior and Lord. There is a difference between calling oneself a Christian and really knowing Jesus and being a follower of Jesus. Many think that, because they were baptized, were born into a Christian family, or have been involved with church in some fashion, there is nothing more they need to do. Wrong! Everyone needs to receive Christ personally and be born again into His kingdom in order to be a true follower of Jesus.

~

There is a difference between calling oneself a Christian and really knowing Jesus and being a follower of Jesus.

~

On a warm day in the early 1980s, during a long cross walk from Warsaw to Czestochowa, Poland, I stopped to rest. My interpreter, an English-speaking Polish schoolteacher, was sitting near me and we were eating as we sat in the grass. People were all about me, when suddenly through the crowd came a young woman who sat down in front of me.

The girl (whose name I soon discovered was Anna) was beautiful. Twenty-four years old, she had lovely clear eyes and short blonde hair. But she sat there with tears running down her face, and—oddly—her legs were covered in blood.

She began talking rapidly.

I asked my interpreter what she was saying.

He explained, "She heard that you know how to find Jesus."

I kept looking at the girl's bleeding legs. I asked, "What's wrong with her legs?"

"Do you see that hill over there and the people climbing up it on their knees?" the interpreter asked. "She has been climbing that hill on her knees to show her love for Christ and has been trying to find Jesus. Someone just told her that the man with the cross knew how to talk with Jesus, so she has come to see if you can tell her how to find Him."

I explained to her, "Jesus loved you before you ever started up that hill, and He loves you now that you have come down. All that blood was not necessary; He has already shed His blood for you. Now, I know He appreciates your desire to show your love, but you don't have to do that to prove you love Him. He can live in your heart."

I explained to her how Christ had died for her and had offered her the gift of salvation. She could pray and invite Jesus into her heart and He would become her Savior.

Through the interpreter, I led Anna in a short prayer.

Before I finished, Anna burst into tears, leaped into my lap, and began to cry, hugging and laughing and smiling. Then she jumped up and started to run away.

"Wait! Come back!" I called.

She turned and said, "I have found Jesus. I found Him. Now I know Him—that is all I need. Now I can go. I've found Him! I've found Him!" And she ran away.

Perhaps like Anna, you, my reader, were raised within some form of Christianity. Let me tell you something: the most important thing in sharing Jesus with others is that you, yourself, know Him. Let me ask you at this point, do you have the assurance that, should you die, you would go to heaven? Should you not have this assurance, then you will never share Jesus in power and consistently. In that case, receive Jesus now and become a true follower of Jesus.

Remember, it's all about Jesus. Whether people already have another religion or have none at all, we are to discuss Jesus and point people to Him and His love and salvation.

IN DEFENSE OF CONVERSION

In this day of "tolerance" and pluralism, the very idea that we would try to persuade someone of another religion to follow Jesus is by many considered to be proof that we are narrow-minded, backward, and probably cruel. Sure, it's okay to try to convert people in other lands to practicing democracy, to treating wives and children differently, to observing human rights, to buying our products, and even to changing sexual practices in order to prevent AIDS. But when it comes to a person's relationship with God, it's hands off.

Even some who follow Jesus (or at least claim to) think that it would be better if we left people of other religions alone. Maybe they are so aware of the prejudice against proselytizing that they are worried about looking bad.

Do we believe that people without Christ are destined for hell, or do we not? Should we not, then the critics are right—there is no necessity for sharing Jesus with others (and maybe not much point in following Him either). But should we believe the Bible when it says that people who have never trusted in Christ are headed for an eternity apart from God, then we must act!

Jesus spoke more about hell than did anyone else in the Bible. Eternity and heaven and hell are not creations of the church; they are central parts of the message of the Bible. We cannot pick and choose which parts of Scripture we are to believe and follow.

As followers of Jesus, we are to care, not only for people's bodies and human rights, but also for their souls and their eternal destinies. A person who cares where another spends eternity truly loves that person! The reason Jesus came to earth was to seek and to save those who are lost.

Whether they are within the church or outside it, people who are critical of trying to convert others don't really have a problem with those like me who go to people of other religions with the message of Jesus; they have a problem with Jesus Himself. He was the one who commanded His followers, "Go into all the world and preach the gospel to every creature" (Mark 16:15). "Every creature" includes the Hindu, the Buddhist, the Muslim, the Jew, the Christian, the tribal worshiper, and people of every other religion and spiritual practice on earth.

The church of Jesus Christ has been a converting church since the beginning. On the Day of Pentecost, God worked a miracle so that "Parthians and Medes and Elamites, those dwelling in Mesopotamia, Judea and

Cappadocia, Pontus and Asia, Phrygia and Pamphylia, Egypt and the parts of Libya adjoining Cyrene, visitors from Rome, both Jews and proselytes, Cretans and Arabs" could hear the followers of Jesus speaking the wonderful works of God and praising God (Acts 2:9-11). Three thousand people were converted, became followers of Jesus, and were baptized that day.

Early believers took the message about Jesus all over the Roman Empire to Jews in the synagogue and pagans in the marketplace. They were so powerful in the Holy Spirit that they shared Jesus in all the known world of the Roman Empire and beyond. As Paul testified, "I thank my God through Jesus Christ for you all, that your faith is spoken of throughout the whole world" (Romans 1:8; see also Colossians 1:4-5).

This explosion of witness and energy took place in the early decades and centuries of the church. Historians tell us that, within one hundred years of Jesus' death, churches flourished in nearly all the Roman provinces and even as far away as India.

We are all beneficiaries of proselytism for Christ. Indeed, every one of us has roots in some place where people were once converted to the faith of Jesus. For example, my wife, Denise, is from England, a land where the people followed the Druid religion before becoming Christians. Many of the Muslim lands, where people are now persecuted for proselytizing for Christ, were once nations where the majority of people were followers of Jesus.

Truth, by its very nature, is exclusive. Certainly we must defend the right of others to choose their religion—

freedom of conscience is a fundamental human right. And we should always show respect for, and never criticize, other religions, even when we see aspects of them that trouble us. We don't want to be negative; we want to be positive. We aren't even really trying to persuade anyone to accept a new religion—we are introducing them to a person: Jesus Christ. Let Him change the way they believe, act, and worship.

"There is one God and one Mediator between God and men, the Man Christ Jesus, who gave Himself a ransom for all" (1 Timothy 2:5-6). Only *one* Mediator for *all*, that's what Jesus is. And that's why we need to tell everyone about Him. God has planted a yearning for Him in every human heart; we are just helping them to satisfy that yearning properly.

The Bible teaches that God first loved us and reached out to us. We are not saved by our own works of righteousness but by the grace of God (Ephesians 2:8-9). Thus it is not our own effort that gains our acceptance but the effort of God in doing what it takes to save us through His Son. We need only to repent and receive Him as Savior and Lord. I make this point because it means we don't have to debate people about their religious views; we only have to share Jesus with them. As we do that, the Holy Spirit will draw them to God.

My fellow follower of Jesus, it is time we not be intimidated by the opinions of critics but instead be filled with the love of God so that we may speak of Jesus and His wonderful life and message. We are bearers of good news!

How beautiful upon the mountains are the feet of him who brings good news, who proclaims peace, who brings glad tidings of good things, who proclaims salvation. (Isaiah 52:7)

∾∾∾

QUESTIONS TO CONSIDER

- In your own words, what is unique about following Jesus?

- Among your friends and acquaintances, which of them are following another religion? How can you share Jesus with them effectively?

12

GETTING
STARTED

*Go home to your friends, and tell them
what great things the Lord has done for
you, and how He has had compassion on
you.*

—Mark 5:19

When we want to catch some fish, we've got
to go where the fish are—or else we're not
going to get a single bite. And likewise,
when we want to be "fishers of men" (as the Scriptures
put it), we've got to go where unbelievers are. So, where
are they? Pretty much everywhere. But they're not in our
little exclusive circles of believers in Jesus.

There are times when we want to get together with
our spiritual brothers and sisters to worship God together. But there are also times when we should be out there
in the world with those in need of knowing Jesus. We
need to make some effort to go where unbelievers are,
and those efforts will be rewarded.

A great place to start sharing Jesus is at home.

Jesus told His disciples, "You shall be witnesses to Me in Jerusalem, and in all Judea and Samaria, and to the end of the earth" (Acts 1:8). That seems like a good pattern for us—starting where we are and in time moving out in greater and greater circles, as God enables us. Our "Jerusalem" is our home, and only after starting there do we go out into the world.

We don't need to go to some far-flung place to find people in need of Jesus; they are all around us. Among the people closest to us—our family members, friends, neighbors, coworkers, and casual contacts—are many who need to know Jesus. We have a responsibility to share Jesus with people who are right next to us and who are spiritually lost without Him.

It's easy. Imagine that next Monday morning a coworker of yours says to you, "Man, my weekend was really bad."

Don't just say you're sorry and get on with your work. Ask him what his troubles are and listen compassionately. Then say, "I'm sorry to hear this, but I'm sure you would not mind my praying for you. God loves you and He cares."

In this chapter I suggest a range of practical ideas you can use in sharing Jesus in your home, from your car, all around town, and with others from your church. My goal is that you will choose some of these ideas, or others like them, and get started with making an impact for Jesus *today.*

SHARING JESUS IN YOUR HOME

Everybody's got a home. It may be a palace, a suburban four-bedroom, a condo, an apartment, a dorm room, a mobile home, or a hut. Even the homeless have a place under a bridge or in a park that they call home. *You've* got a home. So turn your home, whatever it is, into an evangelistic center for Jesus.

Here are some ideas to get you started. They are ways to make use of the contacts you have with people at home through phone calls, mail, and personal contact.

- *Outgoing message.* Let's say you've phoned someone named Sam and gotten his answering machine. Sam's message, delivered in a depressing and grumpy voice, says, "This is Sam. Leave a message if you want to." You're depressed before you even leave your message.

But what if Sam left a very different kind of outgoing message? "God bless you! I'm thrilled you called this number! There are billions of numbers in the world, and yet you dialed mine! God knows you and God loves you. It's hard to get in touch with me but easy to get in touch with Jesus. Hallelujah!" What a difference that would make!

Go, change your phone message now and make an impact for Jesus on all who call you. It's fun and exciting! Change your message every week or so with some refreshing hope and good news.

- *Solicitation phone calls.* Most of us get phone calls from salespeople when we are at home and even at work. When a call like that comes through, we can get mad because our day was interrupted and then proceed to cut off the caller rudely. Or we can consider the call an unexpected opportunity to share Jesus with a stranger.

For example, when a salesperson says, "I'd like to speak with you about our credit card," you've got your opening. Reply to her, "Did you know that you can speak to Jesus?" Or if the caller says, "You may be paying too much for your long distance," you can say, "Yes, but eternal life is free. Jesus loves you."

Be inventive. And be persistent. No matter what the other person says, keep on sharing Jesus with him or her. I have led many to Jesus in this way. You can do the same—all in the comfort of your own home.

- *Encouragement by phone.* You don't have to passively wait for others to call you in order for you to use your phone for Jesus' sake. No. Think of people you know who could use some encouragement. These may be family, friends, or even people you have just met.

Many people in your life are discouraged, lonely, or grieving right now. Call them and encourage them with a message about God's love. Share a Bible verse. Remind them that they can turn their cares over to Jesus. Pray for them over the phone. Should you discover that the person you are speaking with is an unbeliever, lead him or her in a prayer of salvation.

- *Bill paying.* We all have to pay monthly bills for utilities, credit cards, and the like, and it can be a tense time when we think about all the money that's going out. Assuming you're married, that may be a time when you and your spouse say to each other, "Look how much this is!" or "I can't believe you bought one of those." But I've got an idea for you that will revolutionize the bill-paying time in your home.

As you're stuffing the envelope with your check and the payment stub, add in a gospel tract that tells how Jesus saves. And while you're doing it, pray for the clerical worker who will open that envelope and encounter the tract, asking God to open his or her heart to the good news of Jesus. Also, put a sticker that says, "Smile, God loves you," on the outside of the envelope so that everyone who handles the envelope will see it.

Now you'll be happy at bill payment time. You're sending the Word of God along with every check. Before long, every time you get a bill, you'll say, "Hallelujah! Another opportunity to share Jesus!"

- *Junk mail.* Junk mail clogs up our mailboxes every day. We say, "Why do they send me this stuff?" Well, I've got a cure for the junk mail blues.

Go through your junk mail and find all the postage-paid return envelopes. Then stuff a gospel tract in each one and mail it. The recipients are paying to have the Word of God sent to them.

Similarly, you can take advantage of those annoying cards that fall out of every magazine you open. They may include a survey or a request for information about getting a subscription. But these cards, too, have prepaid postage. Put a Jesus sticker on each one, pray, and mail them back.

I have gotten calls and letters from people who have received gospel tracts or stickers in this way (since the stickers and tracts I use have my ministry's address on them). People come to Jesus this way. It's easy—and it's something we can do right in our own homes.

- *Tract rack.* Many people come to your door from time to time, unexpectedly: A neighbor dropping by to tell you about the neighborhood watch meeting; a teenager selling magazine subscriptions; someone with a special deal on lawn care.

Be ready for them by keeping gospel material and tracts near your door, perhaps in a special rack, on a shelf, or in a drawer. These tracts are brochures telling about Jesus and how to receive the new life He offers. You might even keep some inexpensive editions of the New Testament by your door to give out.

When the doorbell rings while you're eating dinner, no longer will your first reaction be to cry, "*Aaargh!*" No. With a tract rack by your front door, when the doorbell rings it will be a race between you and the others in your household as to who can get there first. Opening the door, you will say, "Praise God! I'm glad to see you. We've been praying for somebody to come to our house. Here's the Word of God for you."

- *In-home salespeople.* Don't you love it when a salesperson comes to your door wanting to demonstrate his marvelous new carpet cleaner? Well, maybe you don't—not yet. But you could.

I always invite these salespeople in. And here's what I do when the salesperson starts his spiel. I interrupt him by saying, "Five and five."

He will inevitably ask, "What do you mean by 'five and five'?"

"I'll give you five minutes to talk about whatever you want if afterward you'll give me five minutes to talk."

Usually the salesperson will agree—he wants to make the sale. And I listen patiently while he shampoos my carpet. But when his five minutes are up, I unplug his machine and say, "My turn. If you died right now, where would you spend eternity?"

~

Try this! In five minutes, you can lay out the whole path to knowing Jesus.

~

"Oh, I don't talk about religion."

"You don't have to talk; I'll do the talking. You just listen. I've got four minutes to go."

Try this! In five minutes, you can lay out the whole path to knowing Jesus. And assuming the salesperson has any sense of fairness, he's going to listen, since you listened to him.

You'll get so excited about witnessing that you'll put a sign in your yard that says "All salespeople welcome"!

- *Service people.* When a drain gets clogged at your house, don't think, *Oh no, I've got to have a plumber in here at $60 an hour. I'm going to get him in and out as fast as possible.* No, you should think, *What an opportunity to share Jesus right in my own home!*

When the plumber arrives, have some coffee and cookies ready for him. He won't mind stopping to have a snack and chat with you. Have your gospel material ready and share it with the plumber, asking what you can pray about for him. Then inquire about his relationship with Jesus.

Eagerness to share Jesus will change your attitude toward having to bring in service people to maintain your home. Every time something breaks down, you'll get excited!

- *Barbecue.* Everybody loves a party, so invite all your neighbors over to your house for a party. It could be a Christmas party, an Independence Day celebration, or anything you like. I find that offering a free barbecue works well.

As you get to know your neighbors better in the context of the party, share your experience with Jesus. In this relaxed atmosphere, many will be receptive to what you have to say about Jesus.

- *Balloon.* Too timid to go to your neighbors and share Jesus with them? Then I've got an idea for how you can tell them about your faith and let them come to you. Get a large helium balloon printed with the words "I'm saved. Are you?" and float it over your house.

That will get the attention of your neighbors. The ones who are curious enough will approach you with their questions—and there's your easy opportunity to start talking about Jesus. (Should you have a better idea for sharing the love of Jesus with your neighbors, then do it!)

- *Internet.* The Internet can be a great place to share Jesus with the world. Use your computer now for the glory of God.

Carry on a conversation with an unbeliever by e-mail or IM (instant messaging). There may be unbelievers in your address book already who you can e-mail. Also, you can contact strangers by going to one of the Web sites that help people find online pen pals. Perhaps your pen pal will be someone who needs to know Jesus.

~

You can be a worldwide witness for Jesus right from your own home!

~

In addition, you can take advantage of discussion lists, message boards, guest books, comment forms, and chat rooms to explain who Jesus is, what He has meant to you, and how others can know Him too. Assuming you are Web savvy enough, you might even want to have your own blog or Web site where you present the message about Jesus. Or you can send people a link to www.blessitt.com or one of the other existing Web sites that clearly present the biblical message of salvation.

You can be a worldwide witness for Jesus right from your own home!

SHARING JESUS FROM YOUR CAR

Many of us spend hours every week driving around town in our cars—going to work, taking kids to school, or doing errands. You may never have thought of this, but your car can become a tremendous witnessing tool.

- *Tracts.* Did you know that cars come with built-in tract racks? It's true. Now, some people choose to put their cigarette ashes in there, but nevertheless, automobile manufacturers have supplied cars with receptacles that are just the right size for storing gospel tracts.

What do you do with the tracts in your car? Listen to this.

When you pull up to a toll booth, hand over a tract with your money. At the same time, say, "God bless you. It's such a privilege to stop by here. I used to complain about the high toll; now I'm excited about it. I get to give you the Word of God."

Sharing Jesus changes everything. You'll want to do loops in your car so that you can go through the toll booth plaza over and over again until you have blessed every attendant!

When you drive into a parking lot with an attendant or go through the drive-thru at a fast food restaurant, do the same. Hand over a tract with your money and spend a moment talking with the worker. It ought to be dangerous to be an unsaved cashier at McDonalds, Burger King, or anywhere else you go for fast food, because when you drive there in your car, you are going to share the story of Jesus.

- *Gas stations.* I know it's convenient to use your credit card and pay at the pump for gas, but don't you do it. Hit the Pay Inside button instead, so that you can go inside the gas station and interact with the cashier there. Don't complain about the high price of gas; instead, say, "God bless you! The love of God be with you."

Gas station attendants are often unhappy people. Over and over again, I've had them respond to me, "I hope God does bless me; I need it." That gives me the opportunity to inquire more about the person and pray for him or her right there.

And there's one more thing. Before you leave the gas station, go into the public restroom and leave a tract there. Sometimes I'm so excited that I even unroll the toilet tissue and put Jesus stickers in there!

- *Transportation.* Some people would like to come to church but can't because they don't have a way to get there. Maybe they are elderly and their driving days are over. Maybe they are disabled and are unable to drive. Or maybe they are just too poor to have a car. Whatever the reason, volunteer your car to pick them up.

You can do this on your own as a personal ministry. Or better yet, organize others from your church who are willing to pick up people from their neighborhood who would like to go to church. Match up people who can drive with those who need rides. That way, the church doesn't need to buy a bus or van—you can just use the resources you have.

When you've got strangers in your car, use the traveling time to get to know them better and to discuss Jesus. In the case of those who are not yet followers of Jesus, tell them how they can know Him. Use the extra seats in your car for the glory of God, bringing somebody to Jesus.

SHARING JESUS ALL AROUND TOWN

You interact with people all over town, in all kinds of ways. Think about how you can use these interactions as opportunities to share Jesus.

- *Public places.* Town or city living presents us with lots of unplanned opportunities to meet strangers who need Jesus. For example, when you are at a bus stop waiting for a bus, say to the person waiting next to you, "Hi there. God bless you!"

True, the other person might ignore you. But then again, she might reply, "I sure need a blessing!"

That's your opportunity to say that Jesus knows every person and loves them and that He is ready to hear and answer anyone's prayer to know Him. You can even ask the person to let you have a prayer of blessing for her. Then you can continue and lead her to pray and receive Jesus.

~

Be a blessing and share Jesus wherever you go.

~

In the normal round of life, without going out of our way at all, we meet all kinds of strangers, many of whom do not have Jesus in their hearts. When you're buying a new car, reviewing your coverage with your insurance agent, shopping for groceries, setting up an IRA with your financial adviser, or doing whatever else is on your schedule, don't get so caught up in your task that you overlook the person's greatest need. Be a blessing and share Jesus wherever you go.

- *Restaurant server.* Eating at a sit-down restaurant means we have a guaranteed connection with a stranger, the waiter or waitress who serves us. Don't just be friendly to your server; bring the blessing of Jesus into this person's life.

Let's say you are at a restaurant and you have a wait-ress named Mabel. After Mabel brings your food, say to her, "We're about to bless our meal here, Mabel. Is there anything we could pray with you about? We believe God answers prayer."

You might find out that Mabel is a divorced mom with three kids. She's barely making a living, perpetually behind on her housework, and worried about her kids. She might have plenty you could pray about.

Perhaps Mabel will stay with you to pray. But should she say, "I need to go," you can reply, "Okay, that's fine." Pray for her as you promised. And then, when she comes back to the table, assure her, "We prayed for you and your job" or "We prayed for your daughter who is sick." Often the sense of being prayed for is a rare and touching experience for people.

At this point you can go on to ask, "Mabel, what about you? What's your relationship with God? Do you have the assurance that if you died today you'd go to heaven?"

Your sharing Jesus with Mabel is a greater gift to her than any tip you could leave. (But leave a generous tip, too!)

- *Laundromats.* If you've got some spare time and you don't know what else to do, just go to a Laundromat. With the possible exception of bus stations, Laundromats house the most depressed people you can find anywhere. So walk into a Laundromat, put a big grin on your face, and announce, "It's wonderful to be here!"

People will come up to you and say, "Where'd you get that? Can I have some? How much does it cost?"

That's your cue to say, "God bless you." Hand out "Smile, God loves you" stickers all around. Ask people how you can pray for them. You might be surprised by who you can lead to Jesus and invite to come to church with you on Sunday.

- *Prayer booth.* When your community is having a fair, swap meet, or other well-attended event, set up a table or booth with a sign that says something like "We will pray for your requests." People will be curious and come over to see what you're doing. Some of them will have heavy burdens on their hearts or spiritual needs.

Bless people and ask them how you can pray with them. Probe to find out whether they have a personal relationship with Jesus. Pray for their needs as well as lead them in a prayer to receive Jesus.

- *Garage sale.* It's amazing how many people go to garage sales, isn't it? Even though you may not be particularly interested in selling your unwanted stuff, have a garage sale anyway. Use it as an opportunity to share Jesus with the people who show up. They may get a better "bargain" than they ever dreamed of when they saw your ad in the paper!

Prepare a packet with a small gift and gospel material to give to every person who comes to your sale. Ask to have a prayer of blessing with each person. Then you can ask about their personal relationship with Jesus.

- *Waiting rooms.* Plenty of offices have waiting rooms where the patrons spend time before getting some kind of service. Give people something to flip through besides last month's celebrity gossip or a golf magazine. When you go to your doctor's office, dentist's office, or hair salon, bring magazines that talk about Jesus and leave them on the table.

Don't throw away good Jesus material; recycle it by leaving it where others can read it.

- *Bulletin boards.* You know from chapter six how effective it is to share your personal testimony of Jesus. In addition to sharing that testimony one on one, you can type it up and put it on bulletin boards in public places.

Many supermarkets and other large stores have bulletin boards where people can put up posters and business cards. These can be great places to share about Jesus. Type up your testimony so that it fits on one page, then tack it up. As you make your shopping rounds, you can post the message of Jesus where people can read it at their leisure.

- *"See a need and meet it."* Serving other people is not only a good thing in itself; it also causes them to ask about our motivation. So that's why I like to suggest something I call "see a need and meet it."

A neighbor is sick? Make him a meal or mow his grass.

A mother has been abandoned by her husband? Offer to baby-sit the kids for an afternoon.

A poor family's home is looking run down? Get some friends together and paint the house.

Whatever the need is, serve with joy and gladness. The persons you are helping will ask why you are doing it. That's when you can say that it is because of the love God has put in your heart. You can then go on to share your testimony of how Jesus changed your life and lead them in receiving Jesus.

SHARING JESUS WITH OTHERS FROM YOUR CHURCH

Jesus often sent His disciples out two by two or in groups to minister. That approach works for us, too. Think about other followers of Jesus, particularly ones from your own church, with whom you can share Jesus in your community.

- *Neighbor-to-neighbor community sharing.* Get together in teams of two or three (at least one man and one woman in each team), with a couple of teams moving along either side of a street to share Jesus. Skip the homes with "No Solicitation" signs, but hit every other home you come to. As you smile and present a cheerful attitude, identify yourself with your name and the name of your local church. Extend an invitation for the family living in that home to visit your church.

Then say that you believe in the power of prayer and would like to know what you can pray for them about, such as healing for a sick member of the family. Pray a blessing on the home and pray for the needs mentioned—and for nothing else.

After the prayer of blessing, ask the person at the door about his or her relationship with Jesus: "Do you have the assurance that, were you to die this moment, you would go to heaven?" Share Jesus with this person and invite him or her to pray and receive Jesus as Savior and Lord.

~

*Many people have never had anyone
pray for them in person.*

~

Having a prayer of blessing and prayer for the needs of the family is very powerful and something people will never forget. Many people have never had anyone pray for them in person.

• *Business blessings.* Put together a prayer team from your church (possibly including your pastor) to go to businesses in your neighborhood and pray the blessings of God upon each company and its employees. Call ahead to schedule a time for the team to visit a business. When the time comes, bring with you a certificate that you will present to a company officer to commemorate the event. (You can use a certificate template into which you insert each company's name and the date on which your team visits it.) With as many employees gathered as possible, share about Jesus and then offer a prayer of blessing as well as a prayer of salvation.

- *Apartment complexes, condo associations, and gated communities.* Many of these areas are closed to normal door-to-door ministry by community rules. However, there is a way around these rules that will open the way for powerful sharing. Ask at your church meeting for someone who lives in an apartment, condo, or gated community to volunteer to be the host of a gathering. As a member of the housing area, this person has access to the pool area or clubhouse and can hold events there.

The host should reserve the space and post notices about the special event (maybe even distributing a flyer to every door). Name the party creatively and invite everyone in the housing development to attend. Provide refreshments and perhaps schedule a singing group or guest speaker. Keep the event brief, relaxed, and personal. You can have the host share a testimony about what Jesus has done in his or her life and then have the other speaker share about knowing Jesus and lead in a prayer of blessing and a prayer of salvation.

- *Other ideas.* There are many different ways you can put together ministry teams from your church—you can have youth ministry teams, young adult teams, and senior teams, for instance. There are also many different kinds of ministry these teams can carry out that will be fun and yet be powerful in impact. Here are some additional ideas:

- Prison teams: Visit area prisons, jails, and juvenile detention centers.

- Bus stop teams: Share Jesus and give out gospel materials at bus stops.

- 24/7 Jesus responder teams: Have people on call to meet any area emergency with love, prayer, and physical assistance.

- Bar teams: Send specially trained teams to share Jesus in bars and nightclubs.

- Hospital teams: Share Jesus in hospitals, nursing homes, and retirement centers.

- Mobile chapel teams: Equip a van or bus so that you can perform services at places like truck stops and at special events like auto races.

- Mobile home teams: Contact all the mobile home parks in your area and arrange to hold church services there.

- Follow-up teams: Send small groups to follow up with first-time visitors to your church, with prospects identified by church members, and with new converts and new members.

- Gospel materials team: Distribute gospel tracts and Bibles to hotels, bulletin boards in malls and superstores, hospitals, doctors' offices, and similar locations. Provide display racks and return weekly to refresh the supply.

- Phone team: Offer prayer and encouragement over the phone to people who are hurting or suffering loss.

- Event team: Share Jesus at large public events in your area. Enter a float in a local parade. Set up a prayer booth at a fair or festival. Talk with people at sports and music events.

- "Festival in the Park" team: Stage your own free event in a local park. Arrange for musical groups to perform and for speakers to address the crowd, telling about Jesus.

- Cross team: I don't hold the patent on carrying a cross! A group from your church can do the same thing in your town. Ahead of time, alert church members to the date and the streets where you will be walking so they can prepare a welcome along their street. Information on building a cross and carrying it is found on my website at www.blessitt.com.

ENDLESS OPPORTUNITIES

The ideas I have just shared with you, numerous as they might seem, are still just a start. Maybe you don't even care for some of them and you are thinking, *I can share Jesus better than that.* Then do it! I don't care whether you use my ideas; I just want you to get out there, sharing Jesus regularly and effectively with the people who need Him.

Be creative and think of how Jesus can use you and your church to reach the entire community where you live. Remember, there are no walls. Attempt the seemingly impossible. Pray, discuss, and plan ... then go!

In the name and in the power of Jesus, you are free! Break out of the mold and see the world and its people and opportunities in a new way. I've preached at wrestling matches, porno movie theaters, nightclubs, rock festivals, battlefields ... the opportunities are endless. We should take the message of Jesus *everywhere*.

Start at home. Start today.

∽∾∽

QUESTIONS TO CONSIDER

- Taking into consideration your personality, your lifestyle, and your contacts within your hometown, how will you get started sharing Jesus? Who will help you or hold you accountable?

- What has been the single most important lesson you have learned from this book—and how will it change your life?

ACKNOWLEDGMENTS

I would like to express my deep thanks to my pastor, Bishop Dennis Leonard, and to Michele Leonard at Heritage Christian Center, Denver, Colorado. After I have carried the cross around the world, they have welcomed my wife and me to be a part of this glorious church.

Thanks to the thousands of people at Heritage for attending the training sessions at the church from which much of this book has been drawn. In between our cross walks, Denise and I minister with the church here at Heritage in outreach, training, and missions.

Thanks to the supporters of our ministry who help us in our mission to carry the cross and share Jesus with the world. Your standing with us in support, friendship, and prayers has been the blessing that God has used to send us to all the world.

Most of all, thanks to the Father, to Jesus the Son, and to the Holy Spirit, who have been with me every step around the world and to whom are due all honor and glory. I look forward to that glorious day to come when I will see face to face the beautiful family of followers of Jesus that I have met and prayed with along the journey of my life.

Glory!

ORDERING INFORMATION

You may order additional copies of *Give Me a "J"!* as well as videos and DVDs of Arthur Blessitt's life and journey on foot around the world. Helpful gospel tracts and Jesus stickers are also available. Order direct online by going to www.blessitt.com, by calling (303) 283-7415, or by writing to the following address:

Arthur Blessitt
P.O. Box 201840
Denver, CO 80220
USA

For more information about *Give Me a "J"!* and other items related to this book, such as T-shirts, caps, and armbands, visit www.givemeaj.com.